The Book
of Mormon

Books in the
SkyLight Illuminations Series

The Book of Mormon

Selections Annotated & Explained

Annotation by Jana Riess

Foreword by Phyllis Tickle

Walking Together, Finding the Way
SKYLIGHT PATHS®
PUBLISHING
Woodstock, Vermont

The Book of Mormon:
Selections Annotated & Explained

2005 First Printing

Annotation and introductory material © 2005 by Jana Riess

Library of Congress Cataloging-in-Publication Data

Book of Mormon. Selections.
The book of Mormon : selections annotated & explained / annotation by Jana Riess ; foreword by Phyllis Tickle.
        p. cm. — (SkyLight illuminations series)
Includes bibliographical references.
ISBN 1-59473-076-8
1. Book of Mormon—Criticism, interpretation, etc. I. Riess, Jana. II. Title. III. Series: SkyLight illuminations.
BX8623 2005
289.3'22—dc22   2005012696

10 9 8 7 6 5 4 3 2 1
Manufactured in the United States of America
Grateful acknowledgment is given for permission to reprint "Moroni Burying the Plates" by Tom Lovell, © by Intellectual Reserve, Inc.

SkyLight Paths Publishing is creating a place where people of different spiritual traditions come together for challenge and inspiration, a place where we can help each other understand the mystery that lies at the heart of our existence.

SkyLight Paths sees both believers and seekers as a community that increasingly transcends traditional boundaries of religion and denomination—people wanting to learn from each other, *walking together, finding the way.*

SkyLight Paths, "Walking Together, Finding the Way" and colophon are trademarks of LongHill Partners, Inc., registered in the U.S. Patent and Trademark Office.

Walking Together, Finding the Way
Published by SkyLight Paths Publishing
A Division of LongHill Partners, Inc.
Sunset Farm Offices, Route 4, P.O. Box 237
Woodstock, VT 05091
Tel: (802) 457-4000   Fax: (802) 457-4004
www.skylightpaths.com

Contents ☐

Foreword ☐

Phyllis Tickle

Whether the Book of Mormon is true or not, I do not know; nor is the answer to that question of any great moment here. What matters is that the Book of Mormon is a body of sacred literature.

Within the Abrahamic faiths, of which Mormonism is a branch, a text may become sacred in either of two ways. It can be a direct revelation, by dictation, inscription, or inspiration, from God; or it can be believed by a body of people to be such. In either case, the result is the same, and belief is the requisite component. Belief is a powerful force in us. It so shapes what we are that we become what it is; the object and its reflection in the mirror merge.

There was a time, no doubt, in a less globalized, less intimately populous, less information-saturated world when the beliefs of twelve million of our fellow human beings could be considered of little or no relevance to the other millions of us. The times for such arrogance are long gone … or pray God, may they be. The individuals and groups within humanity determine the whole. We are in aggregate both what we believe and what our fellows believe; and we can know each other in peace and affection only as we know with respect and accuracy what each corps of us clings to as its foundational text.

Jana Riess is an adult convert to Mormonism. As a convert who is also a trained scholar, she has been for more than ten years a clear-voiced and credible explicator of her faith and its traditions. Yet in this present work—the very difficult and danger-fraught one of condensing holy writ—Riess has exceeded even her own earlier work, achieving an apogee of sorts for herself, for Mormonism, and for ecumenism. Of greater pertinence, however, is that you cannot read very far into these pages without accruing benefits from having so cordial and informed a guide as Riess.

It is almost a truism that all sacred texts are initially difficult for the neophyte and/or nonconvert to parse, and the difficulty of the task increases exponentially when that text is narrative. In sacred narrative, unknown characters with obscure and often unpronounceable names wander through strange lands, while having, as they go, encounters with paranormal or celestial or semidivine creatures and even, from time to time, engagements with the deity itself. The Book of Mormon is no different in this regard from any other form of holy writ, but it does have two particularities that distinguish it from other, similar texts.

First, the Book of Mormon contains a greater proportion of narrative over didacticism than do many other scriptures. It certainly has a faster-paced, edgier, more graphically drawn narrative than most. Even more significant, though, is that for American readers, especially American Jewish and non-Mormon Christian readers, the Book of Mormon has an elusive, but maddening familiarity that comes within your grasp, then rushes away.

Much of the foundational story of Mormonism happens in the Americas. Unaccustomed to having a sacred story occur in the Western hemisphere, Americans find this right-down-the-road presence of it to be somewhere between intriguing and disconcerting. Then, of course, there is the worldview and sacred history that are similar but not identical to the Judeo-Christian tradition. Here is an Eve whose actions are of benefit to humanity because they deliver us out from Paradise and into Life so that we at last may do and be and die. Here is a flight from Jerusalem that preceded that other flight we know as the Babylonian Captivity and that preserved the chosen of Israel here in this hemisphere and not in the Middle East. Here are sagas that parallel the Torah and then veer off to stories of kings with familiar names like King Benjamin, whom we feel we must surely know and yet must acknowledge that we do not.

And so it goes but, in this case at least, it goes with Riess glossing the way. Let us be grateful; for it is only when we are blessed with clear passage into the substance of belief that we have any chance at all of piercing through the outer scrims of doctrine and into the hope that is faith for all of us, regardless of our particular communions.

Introduction ☐

My first real encounter with the Book of Mormon was in the summer of 1991, when I was fresh out of college and spending the summer with some friends in Vermont. On a lark, I took a day trip to Sharon, Vermont, the site of the birthplace of Latter-day Saint founder Joseph Smith, Jr. I was not a Mormon and not at all interested in becoming one, but I had done my senior thesis on The Church of Jesus Christ of Latter-day Saints and was curious to see this significant historic site.

Since it was a weekday, the place was not crowded; in fact, during most of my visit I was the only tourist there. This made me fair game for the grandmotherly woman who served as a volunteer missionary guide at the birthplace. She ushered me through the modest exhibit, capably answering my questions while also trying to solicit some information about me. Finally, she came around to the golden question: was I interested in learning more about the LDS Church?

This made me uncomfortable, and I explained that I was happy with my faith and was in fact heading to a Presbyterian seminary that fall to study for the ministry. But she wouldn't let it go. "Have you read the Book of Mormon?" she persisted. I acknowledged that I had read parts of it, since a Mormon friend at Wellesley had given me a copy and I had leafed through it while researching my thesis, but told her that the book simply hadn't "grabbed" me.

"I just don't think you have any right to judge our religion," she declared, "until you have read the Book of Mormon." This statement certainly struck a chord. As a Christian, I had long been irritated with people who believed they knew enough about Christianity to dismiss it without ever bothering to open the Bible. Was I guilty of the same arrogant ignorance? With some misgivings, I filled out a yellow card with my address and agreed to a visit from the Mormon missionaries.

That first meeting with them turned into about two months of weekly visits and dialogue. Because the missionaries were young women near my age, we found that we had a great deal to talk about. But it was religion that dominated our conversations. We read passages aloud from the Book of Mormon and the Bible, talked about LDS history, and debated some of the great questions of theology and faith. I disagreed with them on many points, including the denial of priesthood to women and the Church's conservative politics, but I also discovered aspects of LDS convictions that I found tremendously appealing. The Mormon emphasis on human freedom and universal salvation was attractive to someone itching under the cloak of Calvinism, and I admired the Church's commitment to strong families and close-knit communities.

However, it was the Book of Mormon that I couldn't resist. Somewhere amid all the archaic language and tiresome "it came to pass" constructions (all of which, incidentally, have been edited out of these selections), the book pierced my soul in ways I never would have expected. The immanence of the story, the fact that it answered so many of my spiritual questions, meant that the Book of Mormon began to resonate with my longings. At the end of that summer when I left Vermont, I still had more questions than answers about Mormonism and was not ready to convert. But two years later, after reading the Book of Mormon more thoroughly and studying the Church from almost every angle, I was baptized into the Mormon community.

My story is not all that unusual. Around the globe, twelve million Latter-day Saints—many of whom are first-generation converts—believe that there is something special, something unique, about this book. I am no missionary and am not writing this to persuade people to adopt my religious worldview. If I have a mission, it is one of education and interfaith understanding. I would like non-Mormons to at least sample the Book of Mormon and be enriched by it, the way I have been enlightened by the

Qur'an, the Dhammapada, and other sacred texts of world religions. I think the Book of Mormon has something to offer the world, even—perhaps especially—to people who would never dream of joining the LDS Church.

Evolving LDS Use of the Book of Mormon

The Book of Mormon did not always hold pride of place in Mormonism as a missionary resource or spiritual teacher. Although Mormons today often rehearse the courage and sacrifices of the noble nineteenth-century pioneers and romanticize their religiosity, one area where contemporary Mormons can rest assured that they are not only meeting, but exceeding, their ancestors' example is in their use of the Book of Mormon.

Early Mormons rarely quoted from the book in their speeches and writings; in one nineteenth-century LDS periodical, *Elders' Journal*, the Bible was cited forty times more often than the Book of Mormon.[1] Although early Mormons believed that the book was an authentically ancient record and that its miraculous appearance signaled that they were living in the "latter days," they didn't strongly emphasize its teachings. When the book *was* cited, it was usually to support the belief that the LDS Church was the restoration of Israel.[2] It wasn't until 1961 that a year-long course in the Book of Mormon became required for freshman students at Brigham Young University, and it was the 1980s before the Book of Mormon was cited regularly in General Conference talks by Church leaders. This was due in no small part to the initiative of Ezra Taft Benson, the prophet and Church president at that time, who in April 1986 encouraged Mormons everywhere to read, study, and pray about the Book of Mormon. He echoed Joseph Smith in calling the book the "keystone" of the LDS faith, "the most correct of any book on earth." In the 1980s, the Church began promoting it with a new subtitle: "another testament of Jesus Christ."

That last statement is highly significant. The Book of Mormon is an unapologetically Christ-centered work, its stated purpose being to convince "the Jew and the Gentile that JESUS is the CHRIST." Its essential message, repeated in the text several times, is "come unto Christ."

And that is what Mormons are doing. Their rediscovery of the Book of Mormon in the late twentieth century is strongly connected to their renewed emphasis, beginning in that same era, on the person and nature of Jesus Christ. Mormonism has always been a Christian faith, but it has identified itself with Christ most conspicuously in the last decade. In the late 1990s, for example, the LDS Church changed its logo so that the capitalized words JESUS CHRIST are front and center, easily the most visible element of the institution's name. Even more tellingly, during the entire year of 1971, there were only five images of Christ in the *Ensign*, the Church's official monthly publication for adult members, while in 1999 that number had grown more than twentyfold to 119.[3] Clearly, Mormons are publicly focusing their attention on Christ as never before. Some critics of the Church have accused Mormon leaders of doing this disingenuously, of trying to pass the LDS Church off as just another Christian denomination when it is in fact quite different. But they are missing the point that this theological evolution is occurring at precisely the same time that the Church is looking to the Book of Mormon as never before in its history; the Latter-day Saints' new emphases on Christ and the Book of Mormon are quietly but undeniably interrelated.

The Story of the Book of Mormon

What, then, is the Book of Mormon? Mormons believe that it is a holy work of scripture not only for what it teaches, but for its miraculous provenance. LDS leaders explain that on September 21, 1823, a seventeen-year-old Joseph Smith knelt down in his home in Manchester, New York, and prayed to know his standing before God.[4] He had already experienced a divine answer to prayer about three years earlier when Heavenly Father and Jesus Christ (which Mormons believe are two distinct divine beings) appeared to him in a vision, but he was astonished when this prayer was answered by an angel named Moroni. The angel told Joseph of an ancient record written on gold plates and buried in a nearby hill—plates that he would one day be inspired to translate. This was a record of the ancient inhabitants of this hemisphere, of whom Moroni himself was one; the angel who appeared to Joseph Smith in 1823 had buried the record in the earth at the end of his human life, around 421 CE.

Moroni led Joseph to the same spot every September 21 for four years, giving him instructions and warnings. Finally, in 1827, Joseph was permitted to remove the plates and begin the long work of translation, which he accomplished with help both divine (in the form of a "seer stone" that enabled him to translate an ancient language he had never studied) and human (in the various scribes who took down his dictation). All in all, the process of translation took about two and a half years.[5] The Book of Mormon—so named because Mormon, Moroni's father, was the ancient prophet who edited much of the record—was first published in the spring of 1830. Since that time, more than 120 million copies of the book have been printed in over one hundred languages.

The Book of Mormon is a complex and involved family saga; if it were a novel, it would be on the scale of Herman Wouk or James Michener. It stretches over a thousand years of history and features an enormous cast of characters (some of whom, confusingly enough, share the same name). It's like the Bible in that it's a literary hodgepodge of many different kinds of writings: there are eight letters, numerous allegories, long swaths of narrative history, excerpts from sermons and speeches, at least one psalm, scores of examples of poetry, various snippets from wisdom literature, and an apocalyptic vision.[6] Also like the Bible, it was written and compiled by dozens of people over the course of many centuries, though unlike the Bible it was edited by only a handful of individuals before being lost to the world for over fourteen hundred years.

The Book of Mormon opens around 600 BCE (six hundred years before the usual date ascribed to the birth of Christ and the beginning of the common era), when a prophet named Lehi lived and preached in Jerusalem. Because God had given him a vision of the destruction that was about to befall the city, Lehi encouraged Jerusalem's inhabitants to repent of their sins and turn back to God. This was not a popular message, and Lehi eventually decided to flee the city with his family, including his wife Sariah and several sons and daughters. After years of wandering "in the wilderness," the family journeyed to the Americas by boat and began their own society. (Latter-day Saints do not know exactly where this small civilization was located, but many Mormon apologists point to Central America as a likely nexus.)

All was not well, however, because internal dissension constantly shadowed this attempt at utopia. Lehi's oldest sons, Laman and Lemuel, challenged his authority and bemoaned the loss of their comfortable life in Jerusalem; while one of the younger sons, Nephi, leaned on God in faith and received his own visions that gave him solace and direction. After Lehi's death, his family split quite predictably into two basic factions. The Nephites, many of whom were descendants of Nephi, tried to hold true to God's commandments and to the religion that they brought with them from the old world to the new. Most of the Book of Mormon is their story; as we will see in the text, they often wavered in their religious commitments, succumbing more often than not to pride and sin. At several points in the Book of Mormon, it is their collective foil, the usually barbarous Lamanites, who manage to remain faithful to God's teachings. Throughout the book, these two groups are mostly at war with one another, with one long interlude of peace following a visit from Christ sometime around 34 CE.

As I mentioned earlier, one of the Book of Mormon's most distinctive features is its almost relentless focus on Christ. Even at the beginning of the story, a full six hundred years before the common era, Nephi is given a vision of the Savior's future birth, and Nephite prophets and kings look forward to his coming for centuries before it occurs. The book's literary climax centers around that visit (which only lasts for three days but is the pinnacle of the story), with the dénouement chronicling the Lamanites' gradual annihilation of the Nephites from about 200 to 421 CE.

The Selections

What follows is not a complete version of the Book of Mormon. To be compatible with the other books in the SkyLight Paths Illuminations series, I've had to reduce a 276,000-word narrative to about a tenth of its original size. Although I believe that I have included some of the most noteworthy passages of the Book of Mormon, I am one of those people who cannot stand abridged books in general. When I check out books on tape from the library, I always inspect them carefully to make sure I'm getting the unabridged, complete version.

So it is with considerable sheepishness that I've undertaken this project. The Book of Mormon is one of my favorite books—indeed, for me it is sacred scripture—so there is an element of hubris in presuming to choose its most significant passages. Readers of this edition will find no Jaredites, and indeed no Book of Ether at all; no stripling warriors; no homage to the Three Nephites; and very little blood and gore. (The full-length Book of Mormon is actually fairly R-rated in terms of violence.)

In addition to the usual concerns about cutting favorite passages and scenes, abridging the Book of Mormon is doubly challenging because it's already *been* through a stringent editing process. Since it is the culmination of several different abridgments over the course of centuries, the full text that we now have of the Book of Mormon has already been winnowed and cropped and shaped to its ancient editors' satisfaction. What's more, they followed the rule of all good editors in making sure that the text would speak directly to the concerns of its target audience. But that audience was not the ancient Nephite reader, as we might expect; it was to be the modern reader. It was always to be us. The editors of the Book of Mormon were privileged to peek into the future and glimpse a bit of what the modern world would be like. They tailored their accounts accordingly, choosing some records and passing over many others. Moroni tells us that the current Book of Mormon doesn't represent even a hundredth of all of the records available to him and his fellow editors (Helaman 3:14). They had to make editorial decisions based on what they believed we would need to know. If the result is a book in which war seems to predominate, that's our fault, not theirs. If the book hammers the same basic themes of pride, sin, and repentance, it's because that is the message they believed we would need to hear, however painful.

I have been careful to select those passages that offer insights into contemporary Mormon beliefs and scriptural emphases, such as the Atonement of Christ, the nature of human freedom, the purpose of baptism, and the need for repentance from sin. Through this medley of teachings, spiritual seekers can come to understand some of the basic beliefs and practices that lie at the core of Mormon life.

Acknowledgments

In writing this commentary, I have been particularly indebted to my fellow participants at the annual Book of Mormon Roundtable at Brigham Young University (BYU). This seminar began in 2003 at the instigation of BYU professor and author Mark Thomas and has been a source of great insight into the Book of Mormon. Ultimately, our goal is to help to make some of the research and scholarship that has been done on the Book of Mormon available to the general reader, so I humbly submit this brief commentary as a step in that direction. In particular, I would like to thank seminar participant Grant Hardy for his excellent ideas about shaping these selections, and the feedback he and his wife Heather provided on the Commentary. The University of Illinois Press kindly gave me permission to use Professor Hardy's poetic renditions of key Book of Mormon passages. I also need to thank my friend Ken Kuykendall, who offered helpful feedback on the entire book, and Terryl Givens, who provided important advice in the early stages of this project. I deeply appreciate the willingness of Phyllis Tickle not only to provide the foreword, but to so graciously test the waters of a new sacred text. Since I first had the privilege of working with her in 1999, her openness has been a model for me in interfaith understanding. That interfaith understanding has likewise been modeled for me in my own family by my husband, Phil Smith, and my mother, Phyllis Riess, who daily encourage me with their kindness and support. And of course, I owe my thanks to the good people at SkyLight Paths who have made this project a pleasure: Shelly Angers, Lauren Boivin, Stuart Matlins, Mark Ogilbee, Maura Shaw, Jon Sweeney, and Emily Wichland.

All author proceeds from the sales of this book are being donated in equal parts to two charitable funds administered by The Church of Jesus Christ of Latter-day Saints. The first is the Perpetual Education Fund, which helps LDS young people in Third World countries obtain low-interest loans for higher and vocational education. The second is the LDS Humanitarian Relief fund, which has provided more than half a billion dollars in international aid since the fund's inception in 1985. As King Benjamin suggests in the Book of Mormon, the best way to thank God for his providence and care is to then use whatever resources we have received to care for others (Mosiah 4:16–27).

A Note about Language □

The selections you will find in this book are very close to, but not exactly the same as, what you will find in a contemporary edition of the Book of Mormon. This book was prepared using the 1920 version of the Book of Mormon, which is in the public domain. For these selections, the difference is only about a half-dozen changes between the 1920 and 1981 versions, not including some instances of the word *exceeding* (1920 version) being changed to *exceedingly* in the 1981 version. When the changes are significant enough (such as an additional sentence appearing in the 1981 version of Alma 32:30), I have included a note about the difference in the facing-page commentary. To find references for quotations in the annotations, please see "Notes," where citations are keyed by section title and note number.

Because Mormons exclusively use the term *Old Testament*, which might be offensive to Jewish readers, I have adopted the hybrid term *Old Testament/Hebrew Bible*. When I use the name *New Testament*, it refers to the gospels, letters, and books that, in addition to the Old Testament/Hebrew Bible, help comprise the Christian Bible.

Per Mormon usage, this book uses the terms *Jesus, Christ, the Savior,* and *the Son of God* interchangeably. However, since Mormons typically prefer the more formal title *Christ* (meaning "messiah") to the given name *Jesus,* this book follows that convention. Also, there is a reason why this book does not render God's name in gender-neutral language; in Mormon theology, both God the Father and Christ the Son are considered male personages. Mormons refer to God the Father as "God," "Heavenly Father," and "the Lord" interchangeably, though they most often use the title "Heavenly Father."

The Book of Mormon

An Account Written by the Hand of Mormon upon Plates Taken from the Plates of Nephi

1 Joseph Smith did not write this introductory title page to the Book of Mormon, but translated it from the "very last leaf" of the ancient plates that comprised the record he was led to discover in the 1820s. The original writer was Moroni, the fifth-century final editor of the Book of Mormon. These two brief paragraphs reveal a bit of the history of the record and give a hint of its essential theme: it testifies that Jesus is the Christ, or the Messiah, and is intended to lead readers to Christ. Note that this book of selections does not include any of the materials about the Jaredite people that are mentioned here; for more on them, refer to the Book of Ether in a complete edition of the Book of Mormon.

herefore, it is an abridgment of the record of the people of Nephi, and also of the Lamanites—Written to the Lamanites, who are a remnant of the house of Israel; and also to Jew and Gentile—Written by way of commandment, and also by the spirit of prophecy and of revelation—Written and sealed up, and hid up unto the Lord, that they might not be destroyed—To come forth by the gift and power of God unto the interpretation thereof—Sealed by the hand of Moroni, and hid up unto the Lord, to come forth in due time by way of the Gentile. The interpretation thereof by the gift of God.

An abridgment taken from the Book of Ether also, which is a record of the people of Jared, who were scattered at the time the Lord confounded the language of the people, when they were building a tower to get to heaven—Which is to show unto the remnant of the House of Israel what great things the Lord hath done for their fathers; and that they may know the covenants of the Lord, that they are not cast off forever—And also to the convincing of the Jew and Gentile that JESUS is the CHRIST, the ETERNAL GOD, manifesting himself unto all nations—And now, if there are faults they are the mistakes of men; wherefore, condemn not the things of God, that ye may be found spotless at the judgment-seat of Christ.

Translated by Joseph Smith, Jun.[1]

1 1 Nephi 1:1. It's important to note the very first thing Nephi tells us about himself: he has been born "of goodly parents." He paints Lehi and Sariah, his father and mother, as righteous individuals who dared to defy society's expectations in order to obey God's commands.

Readers of the Book of Mormon should always remember to ask themselves who is speaking, since the book is a complex amalgam of many different authors and editors. Here, history has been written by the winner, Nephi—or is he really the winner? Although Nephi wins the immediate battles against his almost comically unrighteous brothers, Laman and Lemuel, he knows it's a Pyrrhic victory, because by the time of this writing he has been privileged to glimpse the future and knows what is coming. Centuries before it happens, he sees the destruction of his own people, the Nephites, at the hands of his brothers' descendants, the Lamanites. So it's no accident that out of all the many ways he could have opened his narrative, he chooses to reaffirm the fundamental goodness of his parents, whose decisions resulted in the eventual wedge between the brothers.

1 □ The First Book of Nephi

1 Nephi 1

1 I, Nephi, having been born of goodly parents,**1** therefore I was taught somewhat in all the learning of my father; and having seen many afflictions in the course of my days, nevertheless, having been highly favored of the Lord in all my days; yea, having had a great knowledge of the goodness and the mysteries of God, therefore I make a record of my proceedings in my days.

2 Yea, I make a record in the language of my father, which consists of the learning of the Jews and the language of the Egyptians.

3 And I know that the record which I make is true; and I make it with mine own hand; and I make it according to my knowledge.

(continued on page 7)

2 1 Nephi 1:4. The basic time frame of "the first year of the reign of Zedekiah" is around 598 BCE. Babylonian invaders had already made significant inroads into Judah by the time Zedekiah took the throne, and because he was installed by the Babylonian king Nebuchadnezzar as a sort of regional puppet ruler, things only went downhill from there. During Zedekiah's eleven-year reign, many prophets, including Jeremiah, tried to get the people of Jerusalem to repent of their sins and turn back to God so the city would not be destroyed. Their message was not very well received. Note that here and elsewhere in this book, the removal of the phrase "it came to pass that" is signified by an ellipsis (…).

3 1 Nephi 1:5. Lehi, who has presumably heard some of the prophets' predictions of gloom and doom, decides to pray to the Lord on the people's behalf. The sequence is a reliable pattern throughout the Book of Mormon: a person receives revelation only *after* prayer and earnest inquiry. God in the Book of Mormon doesn't typically impart visions or insights out of the blue; he responds to their heartfelt prayers. Here, Lehi prays and has a vision that confirms the fate of Jerusalem should people fail to repent.

4 For ... in the commencement of the first year of the reign of Zedekiah, king of Judah, (my father, Lehi, having dwelt at Jerusalem in all his days); and in that same year there came many prophets, prophesying unto the people that they must repent, or the great city Jerusalem must be destroyed.[2]

5 Wherefore ... my father, Lehi, as he went forth prayed unto the Lord, yea, even with all his heart, in behalf of his people.[3]

6 And ... as he prayed unto the Lord, there came a pillar of fire and dwelt upon a rock before him; and he saw and heard much; and because of the things which he saw and heard he did quake and tremble exceedingly.

7 And ... he returned to his own house at Jerusalem; and he cast himself upon his bed, being overcome with the Spirit and the things which he had seen.

8 And being thus overcome with the Spirit, he was carried away in a vision, even that he saw the heavens open, and he thought he saw God sitting upon his throne, surrounded with numberless concourses of angels in the attitude of singing and praising their God.

9 And ... he saw One descending out of the midst of heaven, and he beheld that his luster was above that of the sun at noon-day.

10 And he also saw twelve others following him, and their brightness did exceed that of the stars in the firmament.

11 And they came down and went forth upon the face of the earth; and the first came and stood before my father, and gave unto him a book, and bade him that he should read.

12 And ... as he read, he was filled with the Spirit of the Lord.

13 And he read, saying: Wo, wo, unto Jerusalem, for I have seen thine abominations! Yea, and many things did my father read concerning

4 | 1 Nephi 1:16. In telling us that he hasn't made a "full account,"
Nephi highlights the first layer of Book of Mormon abridgments: like all
memoirists, he and other writers only recorded a small portion of the
events that occurred in their lives. They geared their narratives for
their perceived audiences and shaped the text accordingly. One of the
most complex aspects of the Book of Mormon is that this process was
repeated again by the book's final editors in the fifth century CE, Mormon and Moroni, who sifted through all the components of the written
text handed down through the centuries and selected only those pieces
that they thought would be most helpful to readers living during and
after the time when the Book of Mormon came forth (i.e., the 1820s
and onward).

Jerusalem—that it should be destroyed, and the inhabitants thereof; many should perish by the sword, and many should be carried away captive into Babylon.

14 And … when my father had read and seen many great and marvelous things, he did exclaim many things unto the Lord; such as: Great and marvelous are thy works, O Lord God Almighty! Thy throne is high in the heavens, and thy power, and goodness, and mercy are over all the inhabitants of the earth, and, because thou art merciful, thou wilt not suffer those who come unto thee that they shall perish!

15 And after this manner was the language of my father in the praising of his God; for his soul did rejoice, and his whole heart was filled, because of the things which he had seen, yea, which the Lord had shown unto him.

16 And now I, Nephi, do not make a full account of the things which my father hath written, for he hath written many things which he saw in visions and in dreams; and he also hath written many things which he prophesied and spake unto his children, of which I shall not make a full account.[4]

17 But I shall make an account of my proceedings in my days. Behold, I make an abridgment of the record of my father, upon plates which I have made with mine own hands; wherefore, after I have abridged the record of my father then will I make an account of mine own life.

18 Therefore, I would that ye should know, that after the Lord had shown so many marvelous things unto my father, Lehi, yea, concerning the destruction of Jerusalem, behold he went forth among the people, and began to prophesy and to declare unto them concerning the things which he had both seen and heard.

19 And … the Jews did mock him because of the things which he testified of them; for he truly testified of their wickedness and their

5 │ 1 Nephi 1:18–19. Like a Book of Mormon Cassandra, Lehi prophesies destruction but is not believed. (And as with Cassandra, his projections come tragically true.)

6 │ 1 Nephi 2:2. The exile of Lehi's family is simultaneously a recapitulation of the Exodus and a harbinger of the devastating exile that is about to befall Judah's people. Lehi's hasty departure, proximity to the Red Sea, extended period of wandering in the wilderness, and internal emigrant dissensions all recall the flight of the Israelites from Egypt, though Lehi is pursued by no one—if the biblical record is any indication, no one, in fact, seems to care at all. Presumably, the people of Jerusalem simply thought themselves well rid of the calamity-obsessed Lehi, whose presence is unrecorded in the Old Testament/Hebrew Bible. Despite Lehi's obscurity, his family's flight stands in stark contrast to the same exile those people would face just a few years later: whereas God led Lehi and Sariah to a new land and provided for their needs, God permitted the remaining Judeans to be carried off into Babylonian exile (see Psalm 137 for a suggestion of the deep pain this divine abandonment caused).

abominations; and he testified that the things which he saw and heard, and also the things which he read in the book, manifested plainly of the coming of the Messiah, and also the redemption of the world.**5**

20 And when the Jews heard these things they were angry with him; yea, even as with the prophets of old, whom they had cast out, and stoned, and slain; and they also sought his life, that they might take it away. But behold, I, Nephi, will show unto you that the tender mercies of the Lord are over all those whom he hath chosen, because of their faith, to make them mighty even unto the power of deliverance.

1 Nephi 2

1 For behold ... the Lord spake unto my father, yea, even in a dream, and said unto him: Blessed art thou Lehi, because of the things which thou hast done; and because thou hast been faithful and declared unto this people the things which I commanded thee, behold, they seek to take away thy life.

2 And ... the Lord commanded my father, even in a dream, that he should take his family and depart into the wilderness.**6**

3 And ... he was obedient unto the word of the Lord, wherefore he did as the Lord commanded him.

4 And ... he departed into the wilderness. And he left his house, and the land of his inheritance, and his gold, and his silver, and his precious things, and took nothing with him, save it were his family, and provisions, and tents, and departed into the wilderness.

5 And he came down by the borders near the shore of the Red Sea; and he traveled in the wilderness in the borders which are nearer the Red Sea; and he did travel in the wilderness with his family, which

7 1 Nephi 2:7. After setting up camp for the first time, Lehi's first act is one of thanksgiving. Despite facing an uncertain future and being uprooted from the comforts of his life, he finds a way to express gratitude for his circumstances and God's provision.

8 1 Nephi 2:14. This is the first of several powerful, moving spiritual manifestations that Laman and Lemuel are privileged to experience—and then seem to forget almost immediately as they recommence their incessant whining. Although it's easy to laugh at Laman and Lemuel (who could be appropriately nicknamed "Lemming," since he always follows his older brother's lead), their obstinacy reflects an important spiritual truth: most people will do and believe whatever keeps them comfortable.

9 1 Nephi 2:16. Again, we see the pattern of prayer preceding revelation. Here, Nephi gets his own spiritual confirmation of his father's teachings, demonstrating an important spiritual tenet of Mormonism: all people are entitled to personal revelation from Heavenly Father about issues pertaining to their own lives and families.

consisted of my mother, Sariah, and my elder brothers, who were Laman, Lemuel, and Sam.

6   And it came to pass that when he had traveled three days in the wilderness, he pitched his tent in a valley by the side of a river of water.

7   And it came to pass that he built an altar of stones, and made an offering unto the Lord, and gave thanks unto the Lord our God.**7**

. . . . .

14   And it came to pass that my father did speak unto them in the valley of Lemuel, with power, being filled with the Spirit, until their frames did shake before him. And he did confound them, that they durst not utter against him; wherefore, they did as he commanded them.**8**

15   And my father dwelt in a tent.

16   And ... I, Nephi, being exceeding young, nevertheless being large in stature, and also having great desires to know of the mysteries of God, wherefore, I did cry unto the Lord; and behold he did visit me, and did soften my heart that I did believe all the words which had been spoken by my father; wherefore, I did not rebel against him like unto my brothers.**9**

17   And I spake unto Sam, making known unto him the things which the Lord had manifested unto me by his Holy Spirit. And ... he believed in my words.

18   But, behold, Laman and Lemuel would not hearken unto my words; and being grieved because of the hardness of their hearts I cried unto the Lord for them.

19   And ... the Lord spake unto me, saying: Blessed art thou, Nephi, because of thy faith, for thou hast sought me diligently, with lowliness of heart.

10 1 Nephi 2:20. This is the first of many if-then constructions in the Book of Mormon. These conditional promises essentially boil down to the basic theme of God's protection and blessings being contingent upon people's striving to keep the commandments. ("Striving" is important to remember here, because Mormons believe that no one is sinless and perfect except Christ and that no human being will ever be able to perfectly keep the commandments in this life. However, they have to try.)

11 1 Nephi 2:22. These particular if-then constructions demonstrate that natural consequences follow from obeying or not obeying God's commandments. Laman and Lemuel are cut off from God's presence because of their stubborn vanity—one might say that they cut *themselves* off from God's presence—while Nephi's faithfulness ensures that he will become a spiritual leader. Laman and Lemuel's ostracism is not God's punishment but the natural consequence of their own decision to reject him.

12 1 Nephi 8:2. In Joel 2:28, the prophet taught that after a time of great destruction, "your old men shall dream dreams, [and] your young men shall see visions." Many Mormons believe that this prophecy was partly fulfilled in the stories of Lehi's dream and Nephi's vision. But since it's nearly impossible to date the writings of the prophet Joel (some scholars claim he was a postexilic prophet, while others place him as early as the ninth century BCE), this is hard to substantiate. Moreover, other key components of that prophecy (e.g., revelations to women and slaves) have no recorded parallel in this part of the Book of Mormon. *(continued on page 16)*

20 And inasmuch as ye shall keep my commandments, ye shall prosper, and shall be led to a land of promise; yea, even a land which I have prepared for you; yea, a land which is choice above all other lands.**10**

21 And inasmuch as thy brethren shall rebel against thee, they shall be cut off from the presence of the Lord.

22 And inasmuch as thou shalt keep my commandments, thou shalt be made a ruler and a teacher over thy brethren.**11**

23 For behold, in that day that they shall rebel against me, I will curse them even with a sore curse, and they shall have no power over thy seed except they shall rebel against me also.

24 And if it so be that they rebel against me, they shall be a scourge unto thy seed, to stir them up in the ways of remembrance.

Lehi's Dream

1 Nephi 8

· · · · ·

2 And ... while my father tarried in the wilderness he spake unto us, saying: Behold, I have dreamed a dream; or, in other words, I have seen a vision.**12**

3 And behold, because of the thing which I have seen, I have reason to rejoice in the Lord because of Nephi and also of Sam; for I have reason to suppose that they, and also many of their seed, will be saved.

4 But behold, Laman and Lemuel, I fear exceedingly because of you; for behold, methought I saw in my dream, a dark and dreary wilderness.

What *is* clear, however, is that the Book of Mormon makes a distinction between dreams and visions. Dreams are shadowy and a bit slippery; Lehi prefaces one recounting with "methought I saw" (verse 4), suggesting the uncertainty of the dream state, and conflates dreaming a dream with seeing a vision (verse 2). Lehi sees the Tree of Life in his allegorical dream, but Nephi, in contrast, is treated to the full vision *and* its symbolic meaning. He also is made to understand the importance of the future coming of Christ.

13 1 Nephi 8:11. The use of the term *white* to describe the fruit is not a racial connotation. Throughout the Book of Mormon, this color is used to symbolize purity and light, a connotation that carries over into holy temples, where Mormons are dressed in white from head to toe.

14 1 Nephi 8:12. Significantly, the first thing that Lehi wants after eating the fruit (which represents the love of God in the allegory) is to share it with his family. In Mormon theology, people receive salvation as individuals, but they attain eternal exaltation (learning to be like God) in family units.

5 And … I saw a man, and he was dressed in a white robe; and he came and stood before me.

6 And … he spake unto me, and bade me follow him.

7 And … as I followed him I beheld myself that I was in a dark and dreary waste.

8 And after I had traveled for the space of many hours in darkness, I began to pray unto the Lord that he would have mercy on me, according to the multitude of his tender mercies.

9 And … after I had prayed unto the Lord I beheld a large and spacious field.

10 And … I beheld a tree, whose fruit was desirable to make one happy.

11 And … I did go forth and partake of the fruit thereof; and I beheld that it was most sweet, above all that I ever before tasted. Yea, and I beheld that the fruit thereof was white, to exceed all the whiteness that I had ever seen.**13**

12 And as I partook of the fruit thereof it filled my soul with exceeding great joy; wherefore, I began to be desirous that my family should partake of it also; for I knew that it was desirable above all other fruit.**14**

13 And as I cast my eyes round about, that perhaps I might discover my family also, I beheld a river of water; and it ran along, and it was near the tree of which I was partaking the fruit.

14 And I looked to behold from whence it came; and I saw the head thereof a little way off; and at the head thereof I beheld your mother Sariah, and Sam, and Nephi; and they stood as if they knew not whither they should go.

15 1 Nephi 8:19. Although Lehi is not taught the full extent of his dream's meaning, Nephi's later vision reveals that the "rod of iron" symbolizes the word of God. Individuals must hold fast to God's commandments, staying on the spiritual path even in times of darkness and trial, if they wish to partake fully of God's love.

15 And ... I beckoned unto them; and I also did say unto them with a loud voice that they should come unto me, and partake of the fruit, which was desirable above all other fruit.

16 And ... they did come unto me and partake of the fruit also.

17 And ... I was desirous that Laman and Lemuel should come and partake of the fruit also; wherefore, I cast mine eyes towards the head of the river, that perhaps I might see them.

18 And ... I saw them, but they would not come unto me and partake of the fruit.

19 And I beheld a rod of iron, and it extended along the bank of the river, and led to the tree by which I stood.**15**

20 And I also beheld a strait and narrow path, which came along by the rod of iron, even to the tree by which I stood; and it also led by the head of the fountain, unto a large and spacious field, as if it had been a world.

21 And I saw numberless concourses of people, many of whom were pressing forward, that they might obtain the path which led unto the tree by which I stood.

22 And ... they did come forth, and commence in the path which led to the tree.

23 And ... there arose a mist of darkness; yea, even an exceeding great mist of darkness, insomuch that they who had commenced in the path did lose their way, that they wandered off and were lost.

24 And ... I beheld others pressing forward, and they came forth and caught hold of the end of the rod of iron; and they did press forward through the mist of darkness, clinging to the rod of iron, even until they did come forth and partake of the fruit of the tree.

16 1 Nephi 8:26. The great and spacious building represents the pride and vanity of the world. Note that the building floats in the air with no sure foundation.

17 1 Nephi 8:34–35. This verse is a key message of the dream: many will fall away. Like the New Testament's Parable of the Sower, which shows the divergent responses that people have to hearing the Word of God, Lehi's dream shows that some people will make it; some will find the tree but later abandon it because they are ashamed; some will get lost along the way; and others will never even try because they are so caught up in the vain things of the world. Lehi personalizes this immediately by bringing his thoughts to Laman and Lemuel in verse 35: his wayward sons, he grieves, will never partake of the fruit.

25 And after they had partaken of the fruit of the tree they did cast their eyes about as if they were ashamed.

26 And I also cast my eyes round about, and beheld, on the other side of the river of water, a great and spacious building; and it stood as it were in the air, high above the earth.[16]

27 And it was filled with people, both old and young, both male and female; and their manner of dress was exceeding fine; and they were in the attitude of mocking and pointing their fingers towards those who had come at and were partaking of the fruit.

28 And after they had tasted of the fruit they were ashamed, because of those that were scoffing at them; and they fell away into forbidden paths and were lost.

29 And now I, Nephi, do not speak all the words of my father.

30 But, to be short in writing, behold, he saw other multitudes pressing forward; and they came and caught hold of the end of the rod of iron; and they did press their way forward, continually holding fast to the rod of iron, until they came forth and fell down and partook of the fruit of the tree.

31 And he also saw other multitudes feeling their way towards that great and spacious building.

32 And ... many were drowned in the depths of the fountain; and many were lost from his view, wandering in strange roads.

33 And great was the multitude that did enter into that strange building. And after they did enter into that building they did point the finger of scorn at me and those that were partaking of the fruit also; but we heeded them not.

34 These are the words of my father: For as many as heeded them, had fallen away.[17]

18 | 1 Nephi 11:1. Although Nephi has heard Lehi's account of the dream, Nephi has to test its spiritual truth for himself, which he does through reflection and prayer. He is spiritually taken to a high mountain, where he receives a detailed vision.

35 And Laman and Lemuel partook not of the fruit, said my father.

36 And ... after my father had spoken all the words of his dream or vision, which were many, he said unto us, because of these things which he saw in a vision, he exceedingly feared for Laman and Lemuel; yea, he feared lest they should be cast off from the presence of the Lord.

37 And he did exhort them then with all the feeling of a tender parent, that they would hearken to his words, that perhaps the Lord would be merciful to them, and not cast them off; yea, my father did preach unto them.

38 And after he had preached unto them, and also prophesied unto them of many things, he bade them to keep the commandments of the Lord; and he did cease speaking unto them.

Nephi's Vision

1 Nephi 11

1 For ... after I had desired to know the things that my father had seen, and believing that the Lord was able to make them known unto me, as I sat pondering in mine heart I was caught away in the Spirit of the Lord, yea, into an exceeding high mountain, which I never had before seen, and upon which I never had before set my foot.**18**

2 And the Spirit said unto me: Behold, what desirest thou?

3 And I said: I desire to behold the things which my father saw.

4 And the Spirit said unto me: Believest thou that thy father saw the tree of which he hath spoken?

5 And I said: Yea, thou knowest that I believe all the words of my father.

19 1 Nephi 11:11. The Holy Ghost (Mormons also use the term *Holy Spirit* or *Spirit*) here temporarily takes the appearance of a man in order to converse with Nephi. In addition to this guise, Christian scripture also records the Spirit taking the form of a dove (Mark 1) or of fire (Acts 2). Mormons believe that the Spirit is the only member of the godhead to not have a physical body; the Father and the Son both have glorified bodies of flesh and bone.

20 1 Nephi 11:13. Again, "white" is used here to symbolize the virgin's purity, not her racial identity.

6 And when I had spoken these words, the Spirit cried with a loud voice, saying: Hosanna to the Lord, the most high God; for he is God over all the earth, yea, even above all. And blessed art thou, Nephi, because thou believest in the Son of the most high God; wherefore, thou shalt behold the things which thou hast desired.

7 And behold this thing shall be given unto thee for a sign, that after thou hast beheld the tree which bore the fruit which thy father tasted, thou shalt also behold a man descending out of heaven, and him shall ye witness; and after ye have witnessed him ye shall bear record that it is the Son of God.

8 And ... the Spirit said unto me: Look! And I looked and beheld a tree; and it was like unto the tree which my father had seen; and the beauty thereof was far beyond, yea, exceeding of all beauty; and the whiteness thereof did exceed the whiteness of the driven snow.

9 And ... after I had seen the tree, I said unto the Spirit: I behold thou hast shown unto me the tree which is precious above all.

10 And he said unto me: What desirest thou?

11 And I said unto him: To know the interpretation thereof—for I spake unto him as a man speaketh; for I beheld that he was in the form of a man; yet nevertheless, I knew that it was the Spirit of the Lord; and he spake unto me as a man speaketh with another.[19]

12 And ... he said unto me: Look! And I looked as if to look upon him, and I saw him not; for he had gone from before my presence.

13 And ... I looked and beheld the great city of Jerusalem, and also other cities. And I beheld the city of Nazareth; and in the city of Nazareth I beheld a virgin, and she was exceedingly fair and white.[20]

14 And ... I saw the heavens open; and an angel came down and stood before me; and he said unto me: Nephi, what beholdest thou?

21 1 Nephi 11:16. The term *condescension* is used twice in Nephi's vision, once to refer to the Father and once to Christ the Son. It depicts the vast love of God and the willingness of Christ to humble himself by being born a helpless infant. God's love, which "sheddeth itself abroad," is offered to all people generously.

22 1 Nephi 11:18–20. Nephi is privileged to glimpse the birth of Christ nearly six hundred years before it happens.

15 And I said unto him: A virgin, most beautiful and fair above all other virgins.

16 And he said unto me: Knowest thou the condescension of God?**21**

17 And I said unto him: I know that he loveth his children; nevertheless, I do not know the meaning of all things.

18 And he said unto me: Behold, the virgin whom thou seest is the mother of the Son of God, after the manner of the flesh.**22**

19 And ... I beheld that she was carried away in the Spirit; and after she had been carried away in the Spirit for the space of a time the angel spake unto me, saying: Look!

20 And I looked and beheld the virgin again, bearing a child in her arms.

21 And the angel said unto me: Behold the Lamb of God, yea, even the Son of the Eternal Father! Knowest thou the meaning of the tree which thy father saw?

22 And I answered him, saying: Yea, it is the love of God, which sheddeth itself abroad in the hearts of the children of men; wherefore, it is the most desirable above all things.

23 And he spake unto me, saying: Yea, and the most joyous to the soul.

24 And after he had said these words, he said unto me: Look! And I looked, and I beheld the Son of God going forth among the children of men; and I saw many fall down at his feet and worship him.

25 And ... I beheld that the rod of iron, which my father had seen, was the word of God, which led to the fountain of living waters, or to the tree of life; which waters are a representation of the love of God; and I also beheld that the tree of life was a representation of the love of God.

26 And the angel said unto me again: Look and behold the condescension of God!

23 1 Nephi 11:27. The prophet who was chosen to pave the way for the Redeemer is John the Baptist, whom Lehi had also identified in 1 Nephi 10.

24 1 Nephi 11:33. Mormons believe that Christ's suffering made possible "the Atonement," or the reconciliation of humanity to God through the forgiveness of sin. Christ's death also broke the bonds of physical death and makes eternal life with God possible. In contrast to other Christian groups, Mormons believe that the Atonement began in the Garden of Gethsemane, when Jesus sweat blood because of his compassionate agony for humanity (see Luke 22:44). The work was completed on the cross.

27 And I looked and beheld the Redeemer of the world, of whom my father had spoken; and I also beheld the prophet who should prepare the way before him. And the Lamb of God went forth and was baptized of him; and after he was baptized, I beheld the heavens open, and the Holy Ghost come down out of heaven and abide upon him in the form of a dove.**23**

28 And I beheld that he went forth ministering unto the people, in power and great glory; and the multitudes were gathered together to hear him; and I beheld that they cast him out from among them.

29 And I also beheld twelve others following him. And ... they were carried away in the Spirit from before my face, and I saw them not.

30 And ... the angel spake unto me again, saying: Look! And I looked, and I beheld the heavens open again, and I saw angels descending upon the children of men; and they did minister unto them.

31 And he spake unto me again, saying: Look! And I looked, and I beheld the Lamb of God going forth among the children of men. And I beheld multitudes of people who were sick, and who were afflicted with all manner of diseases, and with devils and unclean spirits; and the angel spake and showed all these things unto me. And they were healed by the power of the Lamb of God; and the devils and the unclean spirits were cast out.

32 And ... the angel spake unto me again, saying: Look! And I looked and beheld the Lamb of God, that he was taken by the people; yea, the Son of the everlasting God was judged of the world; and I saw and bear record.

33 And I, Nephi, saw that he was lifted up upon the cross and slain for the sins of the world.**24**

25 The Book of Mormon

25   1 Nephi 12:1–2. Now the vision leaves the "old world" of Jerusalem and captures the future of Nephi's descendants in the "New World" where he and his family are about to move. (Many Mormon scholars believe that Nephite civilization was located somewhere in Central or South America, with some later Book of Mormon events happening in what is now North America. However, this is the subject of some debate.)

34 And after he was slain I saw the multitudes of the earth, that they were gathered together to fight against the apostles of the Lamb; for thus were the twelve called by the angel of the Lord.

35 And the multitude of the earth was gathered together; and I beheld that they were in a large and spacious building, like unto the building which my father saw. And the angel of the Lord spake unto me again, saying: Behold the world and the wisdom thereof; yea, behold the house of Israel hath gathered together to fight against the twelve apostles of the Lamb.

36 And ... I saw and bear record, that the great and spacious building was the pride of the world; and it fell, and the fall thereof was exceeding great. And the angel of the Lord spake unto me again, saying: Thus shall be the destruction of all nations, kindreds, tongues, and people, that shall fight against the twelve apostles of the Lamb.

1 Nephi 12

1 And ... the angel said unto me: Look, and behold thy seed, and also the seed of thy brethren. And I looked and beheld the land of promise; and I beheld multitudes of people, yea, even as it were in number as many as the sand of the sea.

2 And ... I beheld multitudes gathered together to battle, one against the other; and I beheld wars, and rumors of wars, and great slaughters with the sword among my people.25

3 And ... I beheld many generations pass away, after the manner of wars and contentions in the land; and I beheld many cities, yea, even that I did not number them.

4 And ... I saw a mist of darkness on the face of the land of promise; and I saw lightnings, and I heard thunderings, and earthquakes, and

26 1 Nephi 12:3–4. In this chapter, we see a kind of microcosm of key Book of Mormon events: the wars between the Nephites (the descendants of those who follow Nephi, probably mixed with other people who are called Nephites because of marriage or political alliance) and the Lamanites (the descendants of Laman and Lemuel, who also likely intermarried and forged alliances with people who were already living in the New World). Nephi sees how their world will be damaged by catastrophic physical devastation in the form of earthquakes and fire before the coming of Christ (here called the "Lamb of God").

27 1 Nephi 12:9. As he did in Jerusalem, Christ chooses twelve disciples from among the Nephites to lead and guide the church. Mormons believe that when Christ spoke in the Gospels of having "other sheep" (John 10:16), he was referring to the Nephites as well as to other groups that broke off from the House of Israel. Although we know little about them, their identity will be revealed in God's time. Today, The Church of Jesus Christ of Latter-day Saints is led by a prophet (who acts as the president of the organization) and twelve apostles.

28 1 Nephi 12:11–12. Nephi sees three generations that hold true to Christ's teachings and ministry, with things starting to fall apart in the fourth generation. After that, the old divisions between Nephite and Lamanite would reassert themselves, and the groups would return to their warmaking.

all manner of tumultuous noises; and I saw the earth and the rocks, that they rent; and I saw mountains tumbling into pieces; and I saw the plains of the earth, that they were broken up; and I saw many cities that they were sunk; and I saw many that they were burned with fire; and I saw many that did tumble to the earth, because of the quaking thereof.**26**

5 And ... after I saw these things, I saw the vapor of darkness, that it passed from off the face of the earth; and behold, I saw multitudes who had fallen because of the great and terrible judgments of the Lord.

6 And I saw the heavens open, and the Lamb of God descending out of heaven; and he came down and showed himself unto them.

7 And I also saw and bear record that the Holy Ghost fell upon twelve others; and they were ordained of God, and chosen.

8 And the angel spake unto me, saying: Behold the twelve disciples of the Lamb, who are chosen to minister unto thy seed.

9 And he said unto me: Thou rememberest the twelve apostles of the Lamb? Behold they are they who shall judge the twelve tribes of Israel; wherefore, the twelve ministers of thy seed shall be judged of them; for ye are of the house of Israel.**27**

10 And these twelve ministers whom thou beholdest shall judge thy seed. And, behold, they are righteous forever; for because of their faith in the Lamb of God their garments are made white in his blood.

11 And the angel said unto me: Look! And I looked, and beheld three generations pass away in righteousness; and their garments were white even like unto the Lamb of God. And the angel said unto me: These are made white in the blood of the Lamb, because of their faith in him.

12 And I, Nephi, also saw many of the fourth generation who passed away in righteousness.**28**

29 1 Nephi 12:19. Painfully enough, Nephi sees the eventual bitter end of his own descendants: because of their pride and wickedness, they will one day be overrun by the Lamanites.

13 And … I saw the multitudes of the earth gathered together.

14 And the angel said unto me: Behold thy seed, and also the seed of thy brethren.

15 And … I looked and beheld the people of my seed gathered together in multitudes against the seed of my brethren; and they were gathered together to battle.

16 And the angel spake unto me, saying: Behold the fountain of filthy water which thy father saw; yea, even the river of which he spake; and the depths thereof are the depths of hell.

17 And the mists of darkness are the temptations of the devil, which blindeth the eyes, and hardeneth the hearts of the children of men, and leadeth them away into broad roads, that they perish and are lost.

18 And the large and spacious building, which thy father saw, is vain imaginations and the pride of the children of men. And a great and a terrible gulf divideth them; yea, even the word of the justice of the Eternal God, and the Messiah who is the Lamb of God, of whom the Holy Ghost beareth record, from the beginning of the world until this time, and from this time henceforth and forever.

19 And while the angel spake these words, I beheld and saw that the seed of my brethren did contend against my seed, according to the word of the angel; and because of the pride of my seed, and the temptations of the devil, I beheld that the seed of my brethren did overpower the people of my seed.29

20 And … I beheld, and saw the people of the seed of my brethren that they had overcome my seed; and they went forth in multitudes upon the face of the land.

30   1 Nephi 17:4. Before embarking for the New World, Lehi and his family journey for eight years in the wilderness. Actually, some LDS scholars estimate based on internal clues in the text that the party covered much of the distance between its first camp and its final destination on the southeastern tip of the Arabian peninsula in less than a year. Their progress was then slowed by hunger, internal strife and bickering, and the consequent loss of divine guidance. However, this is not firmly established in the text itself.

21 And I saw them gathered together in multitudes; and I saw wars and rumors of wars among them; and in wars and rumors of wars I saw many generations pass away.

22 And the angel said unto me: Behold these shall dwindle in unbelief.

23 And … I beheld, after they had dwindled in unbelief they became a dark, and loathsome, and a filthy people, full of idleness and all manner of abominations.

Journey to the New World

1 Nephi 17

. . . . .

4 And we did sojourn for the space of many years, yea, even eight years in the wilderness.**30**

5 And we did come to the land which we called Bountiful, because of its much fruit and also wild honey; and all these things were prepared of the Lord that we might not perish. And we beheld the sea, which we called Irreantum, which, being interpreted, is many waters.

6 And … we did pitch our tents by the seashore; and notwithstanding we had suffered many afflictions and much difficulty, yea, even so much that we cannot write them all, we were exceedingly rejoiced when we came to the seashore; and we called the place Bountiful, because of its much fruit.

7 And … after I, Nephi, had been in the land of Bountiful for the space of many days, the voice of the Lord came unto me, saying: Arise, and get thee into the mountain. And … I arose and went up into the mountain, and cried unto the Lord.

31 1 Nephi 17:7–8. Nephi is able to converse with the Lord directly atop a high mountain (which is reminiscent of Moses receiving the Ten Commandments) and is instructed, despite certain ridicule from his brothers, to build a ship (a scene that will remind readers of Noah from the Old Testament/Hebrew Bible).

32 1 Nephi 17:13. The Lord promises light and direction—*if* Nephi will keep the commandments.

8 And … the Lord spake unto me, saying: Thou shalt construct a ship, after the manner which I shall show thee, that I may carry thy people across these waters.[31]

. . . . .

13 And I will also be your light in the wilderness; and I will prepare the way before you, if it so be that ye shall keep my commandments; wherefore, inasmuch as ye shall keep my commandments ye shall be led towards the promised land; and ye shall know that it is by me that ye are led.[32]

14 Yea, and the Lord said also that: After ye have arrived in the promised land, ye shall know that I, the Lord, am God; and that I, the Lord, did deliver you from destruction; yea, that I did bring you out of the land of Jerusalem.

15 Wherefore, I, Nephi, did strive to keep the commandments of the Lord, and I did exhort my brethren to faithfulness and diligence.

16 And … I did make tools of the ore which I did molten out of the rock.

17 And when my brethren saw that I was about to build a ship, they began to murmur against me, saying: Our brother is a fool, for he thinketh that he can build a ship; yea, and he also thinketh that he can cross these great waters.

18 And thus my brethren did complain against me, and were desirous that they might not labor, for they did not believe that I could build a ship; neither would they believe that I was instructed of the Lord.

. . . . .

50 And I said unto them: If God had commanded me to do all things I could do them. If he should command me that I should say unto this

33 1 Nephi 17:52. After explaining to his doubting brothers that the Lord is powerful enough to help them build a ship, even though they have never built one before, Nephi is protected by the power of the Spirit for several days. His brothers cannot lay a hand on him.

34 1 Nephi 17:55. Having experienced another mighty miracle and manifestation of God's power, Laman and Lemuel "know of a surety" that Nephi is speaking for the Lord. They're even ready to fall down and worship their younger brother. However, as always, Laman and Lemuel's allegiance will not last.

water, be thou earth, it should be earth; and if I should say it, it would be done.

51 And now, if the Lord has such great power, and has wrought so many miracles among the children of men, how is it that he cannot instruct me, that I should build a ship?

52 And ... I, Nephi, said many things unto my brethren, insomuch that they were confounded and could not contend against me; neither durst they lay their hands upon me nor touch me with their fingers, even for the space of many days.**33** Now they durst not do this lest they should wither before me, so powerful was the Spirit of God; and thus it had wrought upon them.

53 And ... that the Lord said unto me: Stretch forth thine hand again unto thy brethren, and they shall not wither before thee, but I will shock them, saith the Lord, and this will I do, that they may know that I am the Lord their God.

54 And ... I stretched forth my hand unto my brethren, and they did not wither before me; but the Lord did shake them, even according to the word which he had spoken.

55 And now, they said: We know of a surety that the Lord is with thee, for we know that it is the power of the Lord that has shaken us. And they fell down before me, and were about to worship me, but I would not suffer them, saying: I am thy brother, yea, even thy younger brother; wherefore, worship the Lord thy God, and honor thy father and thy mother, that thy days may be long in the land which the Lord thy God shall give thee.**34**

1 Nephi 18

1 And ... they did worship the Lord, and did go forth with me; and we did work timbers of curious workmanship. And the Lord did show

35   1 Nephi 18:7. Lehi and Sariah had two more sons (and possibly at least one other unnamed daughter) during their eight-year sojourn in the wilderness. The names they chose for their boys are intriguing. Considering that this is a time when it seems pretty clear that Laman and Lemuel have squandered their birthright as the eldest sons, the parents are aware that there's already a pattern in the family of younger sons subverting the usual order because of their greater degree of righteousness. So it's certainly no accident that these two new boys are named Joseph (after the next-to-youngest son of Jacob, who ruled over all of his brothers because of his spiritual vision— despite their attempt to murder him) and Jacob (the younger twin brother of Esau, who disguised himself as his older brother in order to fool his father Isaac into giving *him* the blessing expected for older sons). In short, the Book of Mormon's Jacob and Joseph are intended as spiritual replacements for older brothers who lost their way.

What's more, the sudden appearance of Jacob and Joseph raises an important question: why are we only hearing about these new sons now, rather than on the occasion of their births somewhere in the wilderness narrative? Perhaps that's because history is about to repeat itself in a way that the Joseph of the book of Genesis would have understood all too well: an attempted fratricide.

As Grant Hardy points out, another intriguing aspect of this section is the relative invisibility of the young brother Joseph in the rest of the Book of Mormon, where he does not feature prominently.

me from time to time after what manner I should work the timbers of the ship.

2 Now I, Nephi, did not work the timbers after the manner which was learned by men, neither did I build the ship after the manner of men; but I did build it after the manner which the Lord had shown unto me; wherefore, it was not after the manner of men.

3 And I, Nephi, did go into the mount oft, and I did pray oft unto the Lord; wherefore the Lord showed unto me great things.

4 And ... after I had finished the ship, according to the word of the Lord, my brethren beheld that it was good, and that the workmanship thereof was exceeding fine; wherefore, they did humble themselves again before the Lord.

5 And ... the voice of the Lord came unto my father, that we should arise and go down into the ship.

6 And ... on the morrow, after we had prepared all things, much fruits and meat from the wilderness, and honey in abundance, and provisions according to that which the Lord had commanded us, we did go down into the ship, with all our loading and our seeds, and whatsoever thing we had brought with us, every one according to his age; wherefore, we did all go down into the ship, with our wives and our children.

7 And now, my father had begat two sons in the wilderness; the elder was called Jacob and the younger Joseph.³⁵

8 And ... after we had all gone down into the ship, and had taken with us our provisions and things which had been commanded us, we did put forth into the sea and were driven forth before the wind towards the promised land.

9 And after we had been driven forth before the wind for the space of many days, behold, my brethren and the sons of Ishmael and also

36   1 Nephi 18:12. The Lord has provided Nephi with a sort of compass (later identified as the *Liahona*) to guide him to the New World. But when the brothers bind Nephi, he can't use the compass, and they are too unrighteous to make it work. No one knows exactly what the Liahona looked like, except that it was a round ball that was small enough to be handled easily by one person, and that it had two spindles that would point the direction to take.

their wives began to make themselves merry, insomuch that they began to dance, and to sing, and to speak with much rudeness, yea, even that they did forget by what power they had been brought thither; yea, they were lifted up unto exceeding rudeness.

10 And I, Nephi, began to fear exceedingly lest the Lord should be angry with us, and smite us because of our iniquity, that we should be swallowed up in the depths of the sea; wherefore, I, Nephi, began to speak to them with much soberness; but behold they were angry with me, saying: We will not that our younger brother shall be a ruler over us.

11 And … Laman and Lemuel did take me and bind me with cords, and they did treat me with much harshness; nevertheless, the Lord did suffer it that he might show forth his power, unto the fulfilling of his word which he had spoken concerning the wicked.

12 And … after they had bound me insomuch that I could not move, the compass, which had been prepared of the Lord, did cease to work.**36**

13 Wherefore, they knew not whither they should steer the ship, insomuch that there arose a great storm, yea, a great and terrible tempest, and we were driven back upon the waters for the space of three days; and they began to be frightened exceedingly lest they should be drowned in the sea; nevertheless they did not loose me.

14 And on the fourth day, which we had been driven back, the tempest began to be exceeding sore.

15 And … we were about to be swallowed up in the depths of the sea. And after we had been driven back upon the waters for the space of four days, my brethren began to see that the judgments of God were upon them, and that they must perish save that they should repent of their iniquities; wherefore, they came unto me, and loosed the bands which were upon my wrist, and behold they had swollen

37   1 Nephi 18:21. Once Nephi is set free, he prays to the Lord to calm the wind and sea, and can steer the ship once again. Although this scene contains some parallels with the Gospel stories of Jesus calming the sea, Nephi does so by praying to God, not from his own power.

exceedingly; and also mine ankles were much swollen, and great was the soreness thereof.

16 Nevertheless, I did look unto my God, and I did praise him all the day long; and I did not murmur against the Lord because of mine afflictions.

17 Now my father, Lehi, had said many things unto them, and also unto the sons of Ishmael; but, behold, they did breathe out much threatenings against anyone that should speak for me; and my parents being stricken in years, and having suffered much grief because of their children, they were brought down, yea, even upon their sick-beds.

18 Because of their grief and much sorrow, and the iniquity of my brethren, they were brought near even to be carried out of this time to meet their God; yea, their grey hairs were about to be brought down to lie low in the dust; yea, even they were near to be cast with sorrow into a watery grave.

19 And Jacob and Joseph also, being young, having need of much nourishment, were grieved because of the afflictions of their mother; and also my wife with her tears and prayers, and also my children, did not soften the hearts of my brethren that they would loose me.

20 And there was nothing save it were the power of God, which threatened them with destruction, could soften their hearts; wherefore, when they saw that they were about to be swallowed up in the depths of the sea they repented of the thing which they had done, insomuch that they loosed me.

21 And ... after they had loosed me, behold, I took the compass, and it did work whither I desired it. And ... I prayed unto the Lord; and after I had prayed the winds did cease, and the storm did cease, and there was a great calm.**37**

38 1 Nephi 18:23. Because of the vagueness of the phrase "many days," we do not know how long the family was at sea. If the text revealed more about the trip's duration, it might be easier to determine their eventual destination simply by calculating the time it might take to get there by sea. As it is, all we know is that they settled somewhere in the Americas.

39 1 Nephi 18:25. Some critics have pointed to the presence of horses and some other animals mentioned here as evidence of the book's nineteenth-century creation. In the Book of Mormon, horses are recorded as already being present in the New World, when most scholars believe that they were unknown in the Americas until the time of Columbus. It is certainly possible that evidence of pre-Columbian horses does exist but has simply not been discovered yet; Mormon apologists have pursued a few promising leads in that area. But it seems more likely that, as some have suggested, "horse" refers to another kind of quadruped that was ridden by humans. We always have to remember that the Book of Mormon is a translated text—a book translated from an ancient document, at that—and so there are undoubtedly going to be some issues arising from that. Perhaps this is the kind of thing that the late prophet Moroni was referring to when he mentions the fact that the Book of Mormon contains some "imperfections" (see Mormon 8:12 and 9:31).

22 And ... I, Nephi, did guide the ship, that we sailed again towards the promised land.

23 And ... after we had sailed for the space of many days we did arrive at the promised land; and we went forth upon the land, and did pitch our tents; and we did call it the promised land.**38**

24 And ... we did begin to till the earth, and we began to plant seeds; yea, we did put all our seeds into the earth, which we had brought from the land of Jerusalem. And it came to pass that they did grow exceedingly; wherefore, we were blessed in abundance.

25 And ... we did find upon the land of promise, as we journeyed in the wilderness, that there were beasts in the forests of every kind, both the cow and the ox, and the ass and the horse, and the goat and the wild goat, and all manner of wild animals, which were for the use of men. And we did find all manner of ore, both of gold, and of silver, and of copper.**39**

. . . . .

1 2 Nephi 2:1. One of the most spiritual discourses of the entire Book of Mormon, these teachings arise in the context of a dying father's words to a young son. In his last days, Lehi imparts counsel to Jacob, his next-to-youngest son, and offers foundational wisdom on human freedom and the role of evil in the world. (It seems that the other brothers are listening in from the edges as well; see verse 14.) Although Jacob is young, one senses that the afflictions he has suffered while growing up in the wilderness have made him sensitive to spiritual questions and open to receiving the "greatness" of God. Lehi promises that God will make all of Jacob's afflictions holy, or consecrated, and that they will ultimately prove beneficial for Jacob's welfare.

2 □ The Second Book of Nephi

Lehi's Last Teachings

2 Nephi 2

1 And now, Jacob, I speak unto you: Thou art my first-born in the days of my tribulation in the wilderness. And behold, in thy childhood thou hast suffered afflictions and much sorrow, because of the rudeness of thy brethren.[1]

2 Nevertheless, Jacob, my first-born in the wilderness, thou knowest the greatness of God; and he shall consecrate thine afflictions for thy gain.

3 Wherefore, thy soul shall be blessed, and thou shalt dwell safely with thy brother, Nephi; and thy days shall be spent in the service of thy God. Wherefore, I know that thou art redeemed, because of the righteousness of thy Redeemer; for thou hast beheld that in the fulness of time he cometh to bring salvation unto men.

4 And thou hast beheld in thy youth his glory; wherefore, thou art blessed even as they unto whom he shall minister in the flesh; for the Spirit is the same, yesterday, today, and forever. And the way is prepared from the fall of man, and salvation is free.

5 And men are instructed sufficiently that they know good from evil. And the law is given unto men. And by the law no flesh is justified; or, by the law men are cut off. Yea, by the temporal law they were cut

2   2 Nephi 2:5–7. Although the law is necessary to teach people right from wrong, it is not enough to "justify" them, or save them eternally. Lehi teaches that only the Holy Messiah, or Christ, can bring redemption, if people are truly humble and repentant.

off; and also, by the spiritual law they perish from that which is good, and become miserable forever.[2]

6 Wherefore, redemption cometh in and through the Holy Messiah; for he is full of grace and truth.

7 Behold, he offereth himself a sacrifice for sin, to answer the ends of the law, unto all those who have a broken heart and a contrite spirit; and unto none else can the ends of the law be answered.

8 Wherefore, how great the importance to make these things known unto the inhabitants of the earth, that they may know that there is no flesh that can dwell in the presence of God, save it be through the merits, and mercy, and grace of the Holy Messiah, who layeth down his life according to the flesh, and taketh it again by the power of the Spirit, that he may bring to pass the resurrection of the dead, being the first that should rise.

9 Wherefore, he is the first-fruits unto God, inasmuch as he shall make intercession for all the children of men; and they that believe in him shall be saved.

10 And because of the intercession for all, all men come unto God; wherefore, they stand in the presence of him to be judged of him according to the truth and holiness which is in him. Wherefore, the ends of the law which the Holy One hath given, unto the inflicting of the punishment which is affixed, which punishment that is affixed is in opposition to that of the happiness which is affixed, to answer the ends of the atonement—

11 For it must needs be, that there is an opposition in all things. If not so, my first-born in the wilderness, righteousness could not be brought to pass, neither wickedness, neither holiness nor misery, neither good nor bad. Wherefore, all things must needs be a compound in one; wherefore, if it should be one body it must needs

3 | 2 Nephi 2:11. This is one of the most beloved doctrines within Mormonism: there must be an opposition in all things. If we have not seen evil, we cannot recognize what is good; if we've never experienced darkness, we will not appreciate the glory of God's light. This essential dualism is repeated some verses later in the story of Adam and Eve (verse 15).

4 | 2 Nephi 2:16. This is a fundamental statement about human *agency*, or free will. Mormons believe that all people are free to act for themselves and can choose God and righteousness. Although Mormons talk about some souls being *foreordained* to fulfill certain tasks—from being the prophet to mothering a particular child—they do not believe in *predestination*, or the idea that humans are merely the instruments of an all-sovereign God who chooses some individuals for salvation and others for possible damnation. Mormons hold that all people are endowed with agency and can choose between good and evil—recognizing, as this verse suggests, that both righteous and evil spiritual forces will seek to influence them.

remain as dead, having no life neither death, nor corruption nor incorruption, happiness nor misery, neither sense nor insensibility.**3**

12 Wherefore, it must needs have been created for a thing of naught; wherefore there would have been no purpose in the end of its creation. Wherefore, this thing must needs destroy the wisdom of God and his eternal purposes, and also the power, and the mercy, and the justice of God.

13 And if ye shall say there is no law, ye shall also say there is no sin. If ye shall say there is no sin, ye shall also say there is no righteousness. And if there be no righteousness there be no happiness. And if there be no righteousness nor happiness there be no punishment nor misery. And if these things are not there is no God. And if there is no God we are not, neither the earth; for there could have been no creation of things, neither to act nor to be acted upon; wherefore, all things must have vanished away.

14 And now, my sons, I speak unto you these things for your profit and learning; for there is a God, and he hath created all things, both the heavens and the earth, and all things that in them are, both things to act and things to be acted upon.

15 And to bring about his eternal purposes in the end of man, after he had created our first parents, and the beasts of the field and the fowls of the air, and in fine, all things which are created, it must needs be that there was an opposition; even the forbidden fruit in opposition to the tree of life; the one being sweet and the other bitter.

16 Wherefore, the Lord God gave unto man that he should act for himself. Wherefore, man could not act for himself save it should be that he was enticed by the one or the other.**4**

17 And I, Lehi, according to the things which I have read, must needs suppose that an angel of God, according to that which is written, had

5 2 Nephi 2:17. In Mormon theology, Satan, or Lucifer, was one of Heavenly Father's firstborn spirit children and is therefore sometimes called a "fallen angel." The Pearl of Great Price, which stands with the Bible, the Book of Mormon, and the Doctrine and Covenants as one of the canonized works of LDS scripture, offers an account of Satan's rebellion. God had created a plan of salvation, to be implemented by his son Jesus Christ, that enabled human beings to retain their agency and choose light over darkness. However, knowing that people would sin and not be able to return to God, Satan rebelled against God by proposing another plan that ensured that not a single soul would be lost. (The catch was that people would have no freedom *not* to obey and would also be forced to worship Satan himself.) Since God's will was clearly to preserve human freedom, agency triumphed, and Satan was banished. But as we can see in the story of Adam and Eve, Satan can still exert strong influence on human beings and attempt to persuade them to his bondage.

6 2 Nephi 2:18. Like the verse above, this one becomes more transparent if we understand the expanded teachings about Adam and Eve that are contained in the Pearl of Great Price. In a nutshell, Mormons believe that Eve made a courageous moral choice in eating the fruit. She recognized that she and Adam could only exist as stagnant children if they remained in the garden: they could never die, and they could never have children themselves. Therefore, they could not progress to eternal life with God. By eating the fruit of the tree of the knowledge of good and evil, Eve brought mortality into the world, with all its accompanying pain, disease, and heartache. But in a sense, she also paved the way for eternal life—not merely the physical immortality that came automatically with living in the Garden of Eden, but a far greater spiritual reward that would enable all people to become like God, their creator, and dwell with him for eternity.

7 2 Nephi 2:20. One of the first things that Adam and Eve do after being exiled from the Garden is to bring forth new life in the form of children. Mormons believe that Adam and Eve were actual people, and the biological ancestors of the entire human race.

fallen from heaven; wherefore, he became a devil, having sought that which was evil before God.⁵

18 And because he had fallen from heaven, and had become miserable forever, he sought also the misery of all mankind. Wherefore, he said unto Eve, yea, even that old serpent, who is the devil, who is the father of all lies, wherefore he said: Partake of the forbidden fruit, and ye shall not die, but ye shall be as God, knowing good and evil.⁶

19 And after Adam and Eve had partaken of the forbidden fruit they were driven out of the garden of Eden, to till the earth.

20 And they have brought forth children; yea, even the family of all the earth.⁷

21 And the days of the children of men were prolonged, according to the will of God, that they might repent while in the flesh; wherefore, their state became a state of probation, and their time was lengthened, according to the commandments which the Lord God gave unto the children of men. For he gave commandment that all men must repent; for he showed unto all men that they were lost, because of the transgression of their parents.

22 And now, behold, if Adam had not transgressed he would not have fallen, but he would have remained in the garden of Eden. And all things which were created must have remained in the same state in which they were after they were created; and they must have remained forever, and had no end.

(continued on page 59)

8 2 Nephi 2:23. It's interesting that the text equates having children with knowing both the greatest joy in life and the greatest misery. Many parents would agree!

9 2 Nephi 2:25. This is another of the most-quoted verses in the entire Book of Mormon. It sums up the reason for "the Fall": Adam and Eve did what they had to do in eating the fruit so that other human beings could have life. Mormons believe that every individual who has ever lived has an immortal soul, or spirit, that existed and even made important choices before this mortal life. In Mormon theology, all spirits have to experience the probationary state of mortality in order to prove their worthiness and mature enough to receive Christ's atonement and eventually return to God in heaven. No spirit can do this, though, without a physical body, despite its limitations, illnesses, and temptations. So Adam and Eve—as we are told in verse 25 with admirable economy—fell that we might "be," or have the blessing of a mortal existence. Moreover, the verse reveals the basic reason why human beings exist: to have joy. Mormons believe true joy arises from coming to understand who we are as God's children and learning to follow his teachings.

10 2 Nephi 2:26–27. People are "free forever" because of Christ's sacrifice. They will still suffer the natural consequences of poor or harmful choices, but they always remain free to choose good or evil for themselves. Note that in the 1981 edition, which Latter-day Saints use today, "mediation" has been changed to "Mediator."

23 And they would have had no children; wherefore they would have remained in a state of innocence, having no joy, for they knew no misery; doing no good, for they knew no sin.**8**

24 But behold, all things have been done in the wisdom of him who knoweth all things.

25 Adam fell that men might be; and men are, that they might have joy.**9**

26 And the Messiah cometh in the fulness of time, that he may redeem the children of men from the fall. And because that they are redeemed from the fall they have become free forever, knowing good from evil; to act for themselves and not to be acted upon, save it be by the punishment of the law at the great and last day, according to the commandments which God hath given.

27 Wherefore, men are free according to the flesh; and all things are given them which are expedient unto man. And they are free to choose liberty and eternal life, through the great mediation of all men, or to choose captivity and death, according to the captivity and power of the devil; for he seeketh that all men might be miserable like unto himself.**10**

28 And now, my sons, I would that ye should look to the great Mediator, and hearken unto his great commandments; and be faithful unto his words, and choose eternal life, according to the will of his Holy Spirit;

29 And not choose eternal death, according to the will of the flesh and the evil which is therein, which giveth the spirit of the devil power to captivate, to bring you down to hell, that he may reign over you in his own kingdom.

30 I have spoken these few words unto you all, my sons, in the last days of my probation; and I have chosen the good part, according to the words of the prophet. And I have none other object save it be the everlasting welfare of your souls. Amen.

11 2 Nephi 4:15. After Lehi offers up some last words of advice to his children and entreats them to follow the Lord, he dies. The rest of this chapter shows a very raw, unguarded Nephi praying to God about his sorrow and the uncertain future. This section is generally referred to as the "Psalm of Nephi" because it has many literary and thematic features that are consistent with the pattern of Hebrew psalms. This poetic rendering of the psalm is taken from Grant Hardy's *The Book of Mormon: A Reader's Edition*; the typical edition of the Book of Mormon just renders it as traditional prose.

12 2 Nephi 4:17. After opening with a statement of praise and revealing how his soul cherishes the words of the scriptures, Nephi utters a heartbroken cry: He is a wretched man! But note what he says here. He doesn't mention his father's death as the wellspring of his anguish, though that would be a natural course given that Lehi has just passed away. Nor does he explicitly lament here that the inevitable is about to come to pass: the unrighteousness of Laman and Lemuel, bereft of their father's staying hand, is about to divide the family. Instead, Nephi's struggles are internal. He's upset with the way he is *responding* to the family's demise. He confesses that he's "easily" beset by sins and that he suffers from temptation. It's interesting that Nephi—who comes across in other portions of the Book of Mormon as the unwaveringly righteous alpha son—records this moment of defenselessness. He *is* righteous, but he also struggles with very human feelings and temptations.

13 2 Nephi 4:19. With the phrase "Nevertheless, I know in whom I have trusted," Nephi reaffirms God's goodness and recounts many specific instances of God's provision and care.

The Psalm of Nephi

2 Nephi 4

. . . . .

15 And upon these I write the things of my soul, and many of the scriptures which are engraven upon the plates of brass.

For my soul delighteth in the scriptures,
    and my heart pondereth them,
    and writeth them for the learning and the profit of my children.[11]
16 Behold, my soul delighteth in the things of the Lord;
    and my heart pondereth continually upon the things which I have
      seen and heard.

17 Nevertheless, notwithstanding the great goodness of the Lord, in showing me his great and marvelous works, my heart exclaimeth:

O wretched man that I am!
    Yea, my heart sorroweth because of my flesh;
    my soul grieveth because of mine iniquities.[12]
18 I am encompassed about,
    because of the temptations and the sins which do so easily beset me.
19 And when I desire to rejoice,
    my heart groaneth because of my sins;
    nevertheless, I know in whom I have trusted.[13]

(continued on page 63)

14 2 Nephi 4:26. Nephi writes that God has granted him spiritual visions, angelic ministrations, protection from enemies, unfathomable love, and mighty answers to prayer. Why, then, does he feel so utterly dejected and alone? This section of Nephi's psalm reflects other elements often found in psalms of lament: physical diminishment and an impossibly heavy heart.

15 2 Nephi 4:27, 29. Although he is generally vague about the particular sins that beset him, Nephi reveals here that he is angry. He also fears, as one commentator put it, that "his own anger interfered with his spiritual peace."

20 My God hath been my support;
> he hath led me through mine afflictions in the wilderness;
> and he hath preserved me upon the waters of the great deep.

21 He hath filled me with his love,
> even unto the consuming of my flesh.

22 He hath confounded mine enemies,
> unto the causing of them to quake before me.

23 Behold, he hath heard my cry by day,
> and he hath given me knowledge by visions in the nighttime.

24 And by day have I waxed bold in mighty prayer before him;
> yea, my voice have I sent up on high;
> and angels came down and ministered unto me.

25 And upon the wings of his Spirit hath my body been carried away
> upon exceeding high mountains.
> And mine eyes have beheld great things,
> yea, even too great for man;
> therefore I was bidden that I should not write them.

26 O then, if I have seen so great things,
> if the Lord in his condescension unto the children of men
> hath visited men in so much mercy,
> why should my heart weep and my soul linger in the valley of sorrow,
> and my flesh waste away,
> and my strength slacken,
> because of mine afflictions?[14]

27 And why should I yield to sin, because of my flesh?
> Yea, why should I give way to temptations,
> that the evil one have place in my heart to destroy my peace and
> afflict my soul?
> Why am I angry because of mine enemy?[15]

28 Awake, my soul! No longer droop in sin.
> Rejoice, O my heart,
> and give place no more for the enemy of my soul.

16   2 Nephi 4:31. Nephi closes his psalm with a clear entreaty that God will deliver him from his own sins and also from the hands of his enemies. Like other psalms of deliverance, this one asks for a shield of protection and closes with a confession of total submission and trust.

29 Do not anger again because of mine enemies.
  Do not slacken my strength because of mine afflictions.
30 Rejoice, O my heart,
    and cry unto the Lord, and say:
    O Lord, I will praise thee forever;
  yea, my soul will rejoice in thee,
    my God, and the rock of my salvation.

31 O Lord, wilt thou redeem my soul?
    Wilt thou deliver me out of the hands of mine enemies?
    Wilt thou make me that I may shake at the appearance of sin?[16]
32 May the gates of hell be shut continually before me,
    because that my heart is broken and my spirit is contrite!
  O Lord, wilt thou not shut the gates of thy righteousness before me,
    that I may walk in the path of the low valley,
    that I may be strict in the plain road!
33 O Lord, wilt thou encircle me around in the robe of thy
      righteousness!
  O Lord, wilt thou make a way for mine escape before mine enemies!
  Wilt thou make my path straight before me!
  Wilt thou not place a stumbling block in my way
    but that thou wouldst clear my way before me,
    and hedge not up my way,
    but the ways of mine enemy.

34 O Lord, I have trusted in thee,
    and I will trust in thee forever.
  I will not put my trust in the arm of flesh;
    for I know that cursed is he that putteth his trust in the arm of
      flesh.
    Yea, cursed is he that putteth his trust in man or maketh flesh
      his arm.

17   2 Nephi 9:3. Here, Nephi has yielded the floor to Jacob, who is speaking to his brothers. This passage helps to explicate the Mormon view of Christ's atonement and the future resurrection of humankind.

18   2 Nephi 9:4. Mormons believe that at the time of the Great Judgment, the spirits of all people will be reunited with their bodies. This physical resurrection is a gift for all that is given solely on the merits of Christ's suffering and resurrection; all people will spend eternity with a perfected body that is free from death and disease. An additional gift of salvation is also available to those who have lived faithfully and received atonement for their individual sins. Those who attain this spiritual gift will be able to live in the fullness of God's presence forever. Thus, Mormons make a distinction between *immortality* (the gift of physical resurrection that is available to all people) and *eternal life* (God's gift to those who strive to obey his commandments and accept his love).

35 Yea, I know that God will give liberally to him that asketh.
    Yea, my God will give me, if I ask not amiss;
    therefore I will lift up my voice unto thee;
        yea, I will cry unto thee,
        my God, the rock of my righteousness.
    Behold, my voice shall forever ascend up unto thee,
        my rock and mine everlasting God.
        Amen.

The Atonement and the Resurrection of the Body

2 Nephi 9

. . . . .

3 Behold, my beloved brethren, I speak unto you these things that ye may rejoice, and lift up your heads forever, because of the blessings which the Lord God shall bestow upon your children.[17]

4 For I know that ye have searched much, many of you, to know of things to come; wherefore I know that ye know that our flesh must waste away and die; nevertheless, in our bodies we shall see God.[18]

5 Yea, I know that ye know that in the body he shall show himself unto those at Jerusalem, from whence we came; for it is expedient that it should be among them; for it behooveth the great Creator that he suffereth himself to become subject unto man in the flesh, and die for all men, that all men might become subject unto him.

6 For as death hath passed upon all men, to fulfil the merciful plan of the great Creator, there must needs be a power of resurrection, and the resurrection must needs come unto man by reason of the fall; and

19 2 Nephi 9:8–9. In other words, without the infinite atonement of Christ, all people would remain in their sins and be fully subject to Satan, who is here called "the father of lies" and "the devil."

the fall came by reason of transgression; and because man became fallen they were cut off from the presence of the Lord.

7 Wherefore, it must needs be an infinite atonement—save it should be an infinite atonement this corruption could not put on incorruption. Wherefore, the first judgment which came upon man must needs have remained to an endless duration. And if so, this flesh must have laid down to rot and to crumble to its mother earth, to rise no more.

8 O the wisdom of God, his mercy and grace! For behold, if the flesh should rise no more our spirits must become subject to that angel who fell from before the presence of the Eternal God, and became the devil, to rise no more.**19**

9 And our spirits must have become like unto him, and we become devils, angels to a devil, to be shut out from the presence of our God, and to remain with the father of lies, in misery, like unto himself; yea, to that being who beguiled our first parents, who transformeth himself nigh unto an angel of light, and stirreth up the children of men unto secret combinations of murder and all manner of secret works of darkness.

10 O how great the goodness of our God, who prepareth a way for our escape from the grasp of this awful monster; yea, that monster, death and hell, which I call the death of the body, and also the death of the spirit.

11 And because of the way of deliverance of our God, the Holy One of Israel, this death, of which I have spoken, which is the temporal, shall deliver up its dead; which death is the grave.

12 And this death of which I have spoken, which is the spiritual death, shall deliver up its dead; which spiritual death is hell; wherefore, death and hell must deliver up their dead, and hell must deliver up its captive spirits, and the grave must deliver up its captive bodies, and

20 2 Nephi 9:10–12. The Mormon concept of hell is quite different from the traditional Christian view. Mormons believe that after death, all people enter the spirit world, which is divided into two spheres: a spirit paradise and a spirit prison. Those in spirit prison—which Mormons may sometimes call "hell"—suffer the consequences of any sins for which they have not repented and have the opportunity to learn about God and decide whether to reject or accept Christ's love and teachings. For Mormons, spirit prison is a temporary place, as almost all individuals who go there will benefit from the eternal perspective that the afterlife has afforded them, and will choose to follow God. After Christ's second coming, each spirit will be joined with its perfected body and be judged for the final time (see verse 12); each will then be sent to spend eternity in one of three paradise kingdoms. A very tiny minority (including those people who have blasphemed the Holy Spirit and have chosen to hate God) will be banished to *outer darkness* with Satan and his minions. Unlike spirit prison, which is a temporary hell-like state, outer darkness lasts forever.

the bodies and the spirits of men will be restored one to the other; and it is by the power of the resurrection of the Holy One of Israel.**20**

13 O how great the plan of our God! For on the other hand, the paradise of God must deliver up the spirits of the righteous, and the grave deliver up the body of the righteous; and the spirit and the body is restored to itself again, and all men become incorruptible, and immortal, and they are living souls, having a perfect knowledge like unto us in the flesh, save it be that our knowledge shall be perfect.

14 Wherefore, we shall have a perfect knowledge of all our guilt, and our uncleanness, and our nakedness; and the righteous shall have a perfect knowledge of their enjoyment, and their righteousness, being clothed with purity, yea, even with the robe of righteousness.

15 And it shall come to pass that when all men shall have passed from this first death unto life, insomuch as they have become immortal, they must appear before the judgment-seat of the Holy One of Israel; and then cometh the judgment, and then must they be judged according to the holy judgment of God.

16 And assuredly, as the Lord liveth, for the Lord God hath spoken it, and it is his eternal word, which cannot pass away, that they who are righteous shall be righteous still, and they who are filthy shall be filthy still; wherefore, they who are filthy are the devil and his angels; and they shall go away into everlasting fire; prepared for them; and their torment is as a lake of fire and brimstone, whose flame ascendeth up forever and ever and has no end.

17 O the greatness and the justice of our God! For he executeth all his words, and they have gone forth out of his mouth, and his law must be fulfilled.

18 But, behold, the righteous, the saints of the Holy One of Israel, they who have believed in the Holy One of Israel, they who have endured

21 2 Nephi 9:25. Mormons believe that people who have never heard Christ's teachings (sometimes called "the gospel" and here called "the law") will not be judged by them. Those who understand the gospel and don't live it, however, are held accountable.

the crosses of the world, and despised the shame of it, they shall inherit the kingdom of God, which was prepared for them from the foundation of the world, and their joy shall be full forever.

19 O the greatness of the mercy of our God, the Holy One of Israel! For he delivereth his saints from that awful monster the devil, and death, and hell, and that lake of fire and brimstone, which is endless torment.

20 O how great the holiness of our God! For he knoweth all things, and there is not anything save he knows it.

21 And he cometh into the world that he may save all men if they will hearken unto his voice; for behold, he suffereth the pains of all men, yea, the pains of every living creature, both men, women, and children, who belong to the family of Adam.

22 And he suffereth this that the resurrection might pass upon all men, that all might stand before him at the great and judgment day.

23 And he commandeth all men that they must repent, and be baptized in his name, having perfect faith in the Holy One of Israel, or they cannot be saved in the kingdom of God.

24 And if they will not repent and believe in his name, and be baptized in his name, and endure to the end, they must be damned; for the Lord God, the Holy One of Israel, has spoken it.

25 Wherefore, he has given a law; and where there is no law given there is no punishment; and where there is no punishment there is no condemnation; and where there is no condemnation the mercies of the Holy One of Israel have claim upon them, because of the atonement; for they are delivered by the power of him.[21]

26 For the atonement satisfieth the demands of his justice upon all those who have not the law given to them, that they are delivered from that awful monster, death and hell, and the devil, and the lake of fire

22 | 2 Nephi 9:29. In Mormonism, knowledge is upheld as a great good, and intelligence is considered the "glory of God" (Doctrine and Covenants 93). However, the Book of Mormon counsels repeatedly against vain pride and people who feel themselves elevated above others simply because they are educated. The main thing, the book teaches, is for knowledge to bring a person closer to humility and to God's love. This is true wisdom.

23 | 2 Nephi 9:30. The Book of Mormon makes many pronouncements against the rich, not because riches are inherently wicked, but because they lead so easily to the pride that causes people to imagine they are superior to others. Riches also engender the kinds of social inequalities and oppression that the Book of Mormon decries. As this verse points out, people can take no material things with them into the next life, so it is far better to focus on the riches that are eternal. See also verse 51.

and brimstone, which is endless torment; and they are restored to that God who gave them breath, which is the Holy One of Israel.

27 But wo unto him that has the law given, yea, that has all the commandments of God, like unto us, and that transgresseth them, and that wasteth the days of his probation, for awful is his state!

28 O that cunning plan of the evil one! O the vainness, and the frailties, and the foolishness of men! When they are learned they think they are wise, and they hearken not unto the counsel of God, for they set it aside, supposing they know of themselves, wherefore, their wisdom is foolishness and it profiteth them not. And they shall perish.

29 But to be learned is good if they hearken unto the counsels of God.[22]

30 But wo unto the rich, who are rich as to the things of the world. For because they are rich they despise the poor, and they persecute the meek, and their hearts are upon their treasures; wherefore, their treasure is their God. And behold, their treasure shall perish with them also.[23]

. . . . .

45 O, my beloved brethren, turn away from your sins; shake off the chains of him that would bind you fast; come unto that God who is the rock of your salvation.

46 Prepare your souls for that glorious day when justice shall be administered unto the righteous, even the day of judgment, that ye may not shrink with awful fear; that ye may not remember your awful guilt in perfectness, and be constrained to exclaim: Holy, holy are thy judgments, O Lord God Almighty—but I know my guilt; I transgressed thy law, and my transgressions are mine; and the devil hath obtained me, that I am a prey to his awful misery.

24 Verses 50 and 51 are almost a verbatim quotation from the prophet Isaiah (see Isaiah 55:1-2 for comparison). This Book of Mormon passage echoes Isaiah's invitation for those who are spiritually thirsty to come to the Lord, who supplies lasting sustenance "without price." This does not mean simply that the spiritual nourishment comes free of charge, but that it is also literally priceless and precious.

47 But behold, my brethren, is it expedient that I should awake you to an awful reality of these things? Would I harrow up your souls if your minds were pure? Would I be plain unto you according to the plainness of the truth if ye were freed from sin?

48 Behold, if ye were holy I would speak unto you of holiness; but as ye are not holy, and ye look upon me as a teacher, it must needs be expedient that I teach you the consequences of sin.

49 Behold, my soul abhorreth sin, and my heart delighteth in righteousness; and I will praise the holy name of my God.

50 Come, my brethren, every one that thirsteth, come ye to the waters; and he that hath no money, come buy and eat; yea, come buy wine and milk without money and without price.

51 Wherefore, do not spend money for that which is of no worth, nor your labor for that which cannot satisfy. Hearken diligently unto me, and remember the words which I have spoken; and come unto the Holy One of Israel, and feast upon that which perisheth not, neither can be corrupted, and let your soul delight in fatness.**24**

. . . . .

1 Jacob 2:1. It's now fifty-five years after Lehi brought his family out of Jerusalem, and Jacob, one of the sons who had been born in the wilderness, assumes leadership after Nephi's death. Unfortunately, his first great speech to the Nephites has to be something of a jeremiad, as they are beginning to slip into sin and pride.

2 Jacob 2:6–7. It's clear that Jacob doesn't relish his role as a stern prophet, pointing out where his people have fallen short of God's law. He is particularly reticent to raise the issues before his listeners' wives and children, whose feelings are "tender and chaste and delicate."

3 □ The Book of Jacob

Nephite Pride, Wealth, and Unauthorized Polygamy

Jacob 2

1 The words which Jacob, the brother of Nephi, spake unto the people of Nephi, after the death of Nephi:**1**

. . . . .

5 But behold, hearken ye unto me, and know that by the help of the all-powerful Creator of heaven and earth I can tell you concerning your thoughts, how that ye are beginning to labor in sin, which sin appeareth very abominable unto me, yea, and abominable unto God.

6 Yea, it grieveth my soul and causeth me to shrink with shame before the presence of my Maker, that I might testify unto you concerning the wickedness of your hearts.**2**

7 And also it grieveth me that I must use so much boldness of speech concerning you, before your wives and your children, many of whose feelings are exceedingly tender and chaste and delicate before God, which thing is pleasing unto God;

. . . . .

12 And now behold, my brethren, this is the word which I declare unto you, that many of you have begun to search for gold, and for silver, and for all manner of precious ores, in the which this land, which is

3　Jacob 2:13. Jacob hammers home one of the Book of Mormon's main spiritual themes: that pride in riches is vain and sinful. The Book of Mormon teaches that wealth (and in particular, an unequal distribution of wealth) often leads to other serious sins.

4　Jacob 2:23. The Nephites' riches have led to "grosser crimes," including sexual immorality. Considering the importance of polygamy (also called plural marriage) in nineteenth-century Mormonism, this passage surprises both Mormon and non-Mormon readers. Apparently, Nephite men were engaging in "whoredoms"—that is, having sexual intercourse with women who were not their wives—and trying to justify it on the basis of the polygamous precedent of Hebrew Bible/Old Testament figures like David and Solomon. But Jacob is clear that if the Nephites imagine that they can simply excuse their own immoral behavior by drawing on biblical precedent, they "understand not the scriptures."

5　Jacob 2:24. The fact that David and Solomon had many wives and concubines was "abominable" to the Lord, Jacob declares. So if the Nephites think that their actions are validated by the actions of those biblical kings, they are dead wrong.

a land of promise unto you and to your seed, doth abound most plentifully.

13 And the hand of providence hath smiled upon you most pleasingly, that you have obtained many riches; and because some of you have obtained more abundantly than that of your brethren ye are lifted up in the pride of your hearts, and wear stiff necks and high heads because of the costliness of your apparel, and persecute your brethren because ye suppose that ye are better than they.[3]

. . . . .

22 And now I make an end of speaking unto you concerning this pride. And were it not that I must speak unto you concerning a grosser crime, my heart would rejoice exceedingly because of you.

23 But the word of God burdens me because of your grosser crimes. For behold, thus saith the Lord: This people begin to wax in iniquity; they understand not the scriptures, for they seek to excuse themselves in committing whoredoms, because of the things which were written concerning David, and Solomon his son.[4]

24 Behold, David and Solomon truly had many wives and concubines, which thing was abominable before me, saith the Lord.[5]

25 Wherefore, thus saith the Lord, I have led this people forth out of the land of Jerusalem, by the power of mine arm, that I might raise up unto me a righteous branch from the fruit of the loins of Joseph.

26 Wherefore, I the Lord God will not suffer that this people shall do like unto them of old.

(continued on page 83)

6 | Jacob 2:27. Jacob could not be clearer in his meaning: Men may have one wife and no concubines. God demands total sexual fidelity within marriage.

7 | Jacob 2:30. This is the key verse for understanding why Mormons believe that Joseph Smith, Brigham Young, and other nineteenth-century Mormons were justified in their practice of polygamy, but that this is the exception to the Lord's law, not the rule. Here, God states that if he ever does wish to institute plural marriage for the purpose of raising up seed (i.e., enabling men to have more children than they could if married to only one wife), he will make that clear by way of a specific commandment. Mormons believe that the Lord did just that in the 1830s, when Joseph Smith quietly began the practice of plural marriage. The revelation that commanded it was recorded in 1843, but the Mormons did not make their polygamous relationships public knowledge until 1852. Polygamy was officially practiced by the Latter-day Saints until 1890, when Mormon prophet Wilford Woodruff ceded to government pressure and said that the Mormons would obey the law of the land. Because some Mormons were loathe to abandon the practice and continued to secretly contract new plural marriages, the Church issued an uncompromising statement in 1904 that stipulated that any Mormon found to be practicing polygamy would be excommunicated. That has remained the Church's policy for a hundred years; although there are some offshoot groups that still practice polygamy, members of those groups are not affiliated with The Church of Jesus Christ of Latter-day Saints. Mormons believe that the period when polygamy was publicly sanctioned (1852–1890)—and the longer period in which it was privately approved (the early 1830s to 1904)—were exceptions to God's basic law that Jacob spelled out in verse 27.

8 | Jacob 2:31–32. Polygamy, Jacob says, breaks women's hearts. God has seen the sorrow and suffering of Nephite wives whose husbands were disobeying the commandments by *(continued on page 84)*

27 Wherefore, my brethren, hear me, and hearken to the word of the Lord: For there shall not any man among you have save it be one wife; and concubines he shall have none;**6**

28 For I, the Lord God, delight in the chastity of women. And whoredoms are an abomination before me; thus saith the Lord of Hosts.

29 Wherefore, this people shall keep my commandments, saith the Lord of Hosts, or cursed be the land for their sakes.

30 For if I will, saith the Lord of Hosts, raise up seed unto me, I will command my people; otherwise they shall hearken unto these things.**7**

31 For behold, I, the Lord, have seen the sorrow, and heard the mourning of the daughters of my people in the land of Jerusalem, yea, and in all the lands of my people, because of the wickedness and abominations of their husbands.

32 And I will not suffer, saith the Lord of Hosts, that the cries of the fair daughters of this people, which I have led out of the land of Jerusalem, shall come up unto me against the men of my people, saith the Lord of Hosts.**8**

33 For they shall not lead away captive the daughters of my people because of their tenderness, save I shall visit them with a sore curse, even unto destruction; for they shall not commit whoredoms, like unto them of old, saith the Lord of Hosts.

(continued on page 85)

taking other wives and concubines, and God says he will not allow these women's cries to go unanswered.

9 Jacob 2:34. As is stated elsewhere in the Book of Mormon, people aren't punished for breaking laws they didn't know about. However, they will be held accountable for disobeying God's commandments when they know full well what those commandments require—as is the case with these second- and third-generation descendants of Lehi.

10 Jacob 5:1. Mormons believe that Zenos was an ancient prophet in Israel or Judah whose writings were ultimately not included in the canon of the Old Testament/Hebrew Bible, though they were preserved in the brass plates that Lehi and his family had brought with them from Jerusalem. Here, Jacob quotes Zenos's extended allegory of the tame and wild olive trees—a reference to Israel and the Gentiles.

11 Jacob 5:3–4. Note the care with which the gardener (God) cares for the tame olive tree (Israel). When he sees signs of decay, he prunes, digs, and nourishes to save the tree.

34 And now behold, my brethren, ye know that these commandments were given to our father, Lehi; wherefore, ye have known them before; and ye have come unto great condemnation; for ye have done these things which ye ought not to have done.**9**

35 Behold, ye have done greater iniquities than the Lamanites, our brethren. Ye have broken the hearts of your tender wives, and lost the confidence of your children, because of your bad examples before them; and the sobbings of their hearts ascend up to God against you. And because of the strictness of the word of God, which cometh down against you, many hearts died, pierced with deep wounds.

The Allegory of the Olive Tree

Jacob 5

1 Behold, my brethren, do ye not remember to have read the words of the prophet Zenos,**10** which he spake unto the house of Israel, saying:

2 Hearken, O ye house of Israel, and hear the words of me, a prophet of the Lord.

3 For behold, thus saith the Lord, I will liken thee, O house of Israel, like unto a tame olive-tree, which a man took and nourished in his vineyard; and it grew, and waxed old, and began to decay.

4 And ... the master of the vineyard went forth, and he saw that his olive-tree began to decay; and he said: I will prune it, and dig about it, and nourish it, that perhaps it may shoot forth young and tender branches, and it perish not.**11**

5 And ... he pruned it, and digged about it, and nourished it according to his word.

12 Jacob 5:6. The "main top" of the tree that is beginning to decay may represent the leadership of Israel. Decay symbolizes *apostasy*, or falling away from the truth.

13 Jacob 5:7: The servant is the Savior, or God's son Jesus Christ.

14 Jacob 5:7. As a desperate measure, the gardener decides to perform a kind of botanical surgery on the tree by grafting in the branches of a wild olive tree to revive the tame one. The wild branches represent the Gentiles, who have a role in preserving God's people of Israel. It is clear from this verse and others that God feels great pain at the thought that Israel might be lost to him.

6 And ... after many days it began to put forth somewhat a little, young and tender branches; but behold, the main top thereof began to perish.[12]

7 And ... the master of the vineyard saw it, and he said unto his servant[13]: It grieveth me that I should lose this tree; wherefore, go and pluck the branches from a wild olive-tree, and bring them hither unto me; and we will pluck off those main branches which are beginning to wither away, and we will cast them into the fire that they may be burned.[14]

8 And behold, saith the Lord of the vineyard, I take away many of these young and tender branches, and I will graft them whithersoever I will; and it mattereth not that if it so be that the root of this tree will perish, I may preserve the fruit thereof unto myself; wherefore, I will take these young and tender branches, and I will graft them whithersoever I will.

9 Take thou the branches of the wild olive-tree, and graft them in, in the stead thereof; and these which I have plucked off I will cast into the fire and burn them, that they may not cumber the ground of my vineyard.

10 And ... the servant of the Lord of the vineyard did according to the word of the Lord of the vineyard, and grafted in the branches of the wild olive-tree.

11 And the Lord of the vineyard caused that it should be digged about, and pruned, and nourished, saying unto his servant: It grieveth me that I should lose this tree; wherefore, that perhaps I might preserve the roots thereof that they perish not, that I might preserve them unto myself, I have done this thing.

12 Wherefore, go thy way; watch the tree, and nourish it, according to my words.

15　Jacob 5:13. The tame olive trees are placed in the "nethermost part" of the vineyard to preserve them. This represents the *diaspora* (scattering) of Israel throughout the world. The Book of Mormon itself is the result of God's "scattering" of Lehi and his family to the New World; the presence of Zenos's prophecy here when it is preserved in no other place also demonstrates God's desire to keep Israel's teachings intact. Mormons believe that other righteous remnants of the house of Israel are also located in various places throughout the world and that they have their own ancient records.

16　Jacob 5:15. "A long time": the allegory then skips ahead hundreds of years to the coming of Christ. Here, the servant laboring in the vineyard is Christ, teaching and ministering to the people. Interestingly, the master of the vineyard (God) is there with him.

17　Jacob 5:17–18. At long last, the master and the servant begin to see the fruit of their labors. The grafted tree is thriving; in fact, its roots are stronger than they would have been without the graft from the wild olive tree. (Apparently, some of the Gentile converts of the first century were aware of their contribution to this revitalization, which led to Paul's soft rebuke in Romans 11:17–18: "if you … a wild olive shoot, were grafted in their place to share the rich root of the olive tree, do not boast over the branches. If you do boast, remember that it is not you that support the root, but the root that supports you." (Although Mormons routinely use the King James Version, this is from the NRSV, which is a more accessible translation of this passage.)

13 And these will I place in the nethermost part[15] of my vineyard, whithersoever I will, it mattereth not unto thee; and I do it that I may preserve unto myself the natural branches of the tree; and also, that I may lay up fruit thereof against the season, unto myself; for it grieveth me that I should lose this tree and the fruit thereof.

14 And ... the Lord of the vineyard went his way, and hid the natural branches of the tame olive-tree in the nethermost parts of the vineyard, some in one and some in another, according to his will and pleasure.

15 And ... a long time[16] passed away, and the Lord of the vineyard said unto his servant: Come, let us go down into the vineyard, that we may labor in the vineyard.

16 And ... the Lord of the vineyard, and also the servant, went down into the vineyard to labor. And ... the servant said unto his master: Behold, look here; behold the tree.

17 And ... the Lord of the vineyard looked and beheld the tree in the which the wild olive branches had been grafted; and it had sprung forth and begun to bear fruit. And he beheld that it was good; and the fruit thereof was like unto the natural fruit.

18 And he said unto the servant: Behold, the branches of the wild tree have taken hold of the moisture of the root thereof, that the root thereof hath brought forth much strength; and because of the much strength of the root thereof the wild branches have brought forth tame fruit. Now, if we had not grafted in these branches, the tree thereof would have perished. And now, behold, I shall lay up much fruit, which the tree thereof hath brought forth; and the fruit thereof I shall lay up against the season, unto mine own self.[17]

19 And ... the Lord of the vineyard said unto the servant: Come, let us go to the nethermost part of the vineyard, and behold if the natural

18 Jacob 5:19. The master of the vineyard and his servant go to check on the other trees they've planted in the nethermost part of the vineyard. Most seem to be thriving, even one that grew in very poor ground. Here, Zenos teaches that after his ministry in and around Jerusalem, Christ will visit his "other sheep" in other parts of the world.

branches of the tree have not brought forth much fruit also, that I may lay up of the fruit thereof against the season, unto mine own self.**18**

20 And ... they went forth whither the master had hid the natural branches of the tree, and he said unto the servant: Behold these; and he beheld the first that it had brought forth much fruit; and he beheld also that it was good. And he said unto the servant: Take of the fruit thereof, and lay it up against the season, that I may preserve it unto mine own self; for behold, said he, this long time have I nourished it, and it hath brought forth much fruit.

21 And ... the servant said unto his master: How comest thou hither to plant this tree, or this branch of the tree? For behold, it was the poorest spot in all the land of thy vineyard.

22 And the Lord of the vineyard said unto him: Counsel me not; I knew that it was a poor spot of ground; wherefore, I said unto thee, I have nourished it this long time, and thou beholdest that it hath brought forth much fruit.

23 And ... the Lord of the vineyard said unto his servant: Look hither; behold I have planted another branch of the tree also; and thou knowest that this spot of ground was poorer than the first. But, behold the tree. I have nourished it this long time, and it hath brought forth much fruit; therefore, gather it, and lay it up against the season, that I may preserve it unto mine own self.

24 And ... the Lord of the vineyard said again unto his servant: Look hither, and behold another branch also, which I have planted; behold that I have nourished it also, and it hath brought forth fruit.

25 And he said unto the servant: Look hither and behold the last. Behold, this have I planted in a good spot of ground; and I have nourished it this long time, and only a part of the tree hath brought

19 Jacob 5:25. This last "tree" of scattered Israel represents Lehi and his descendants in the New World. Although it has been planted in a good spot of ground and the master of the vineyard has nourished it continually, only a part of the tree bears tame fruit. On first glance, this would seem to symbolize the split between the Nephites, who brought forth good fruit, and the Lamanites, who did not. However, a closer reading of the Book of Mormon suggests that the reality was far more complex. Many of the Lamanites whose stories were recorded in the Book of Mormon were righteous, and many of the Nephites succumbed to pride, vanity, selfishness, and hatred. Also, the first few generations after Christ's visit saw considerable intermingling of both peoples, with the former divisions set aside for a time.

20 Jacob 5:27. The servant (Christ) pleads on behalf of the unrighteous people in the New World, encouraging God to nurture them a little longer.

21 Jacob 5:29–32. This section refers to what Mormons call "the Great Apostasy," that time several generations after Christ when they believe the leadership of the church in Jerusalem began to fall away from the true gospel. Although the mother tree (Israel) has borne a great deal of fruit, it is not *good* fruit. For the third time, the allegory records the grief of the master gardener.

forth tame fruit, and the other part of the tree hath brought forth wild fruit; behold, I have nourished this tree like unto the others.**19**

26 And ... the Lord of the vineyard said unto the servant: Pluck off the branches that have not brought forth good fruit, and cast them into the fire.

27 But behold, the servant said unto him: Let us prune it, and dig about it, and nourish it a little longer, that perhaps it may bring forth good fruit unto thee, that thou canst lay it up against the season.**20**

28 And ... the Lord of the vineyard and the servant of the Lord of the vineyard did nourish all the fruit of the vineyard.

29 And ... a long time had passed away, and the Lord of the vineyard said unto his servant: Come, let us go down into the vineyard, that we may labor again in the vineyard. For behold, the time draweth near, and the end soon cometh; wherefore, I must lay up fruit against the season, unto mine own self.

30 And ... the Lord of the vineyard and the servant went down into the vineyard; and they came to the tree whose natural branches had been broken off, and the wild branches had been grafted in; and behold all sorts of fruit did cumber the tree.

31 And ... the Lord of the vineyard did taste of the fruit, every sort according to its number. And the Lord of the vineyard said: Behold, this long time have we nourished this tree, and I have laid up unto myself against the season much fruit.

32 But behold, this time it hath brought forth much fruit, and there is none of it which is good. And behold, there are all kinds of bad fruit; and it profiteth me nothing, notwithstanding all our labor; and now it grieveth me that I should lose this tree.**21**

22 Jacob 5:39. After their terrible disappointment with the mother tree, the gardener and his servant are also dismayed to discover that the trees they planted in the nethermost parts of the vineyard have gone bad as well. For the Nephites and Lamanites, this represents the apostasy of both groups, because the "wild part" of their tree (the unrighteous people, consisting of primarily Lamanites) had overcome the part that had brought forth good fruit (mostly Nephites).

33 And the Lord of the vineyard said unto the servant: What shall we do unto the tree, that I may preserve again good fruit thereof unto mine own self?

34 And the servant said unto his master: Behold, because thou didst graft in the branches of the wild olive-tree they have nourished the roots, that they are alive and they have not perished; wherefore thou beholdest that they are yet good.

35 And ... the Lord of the vineyard said unto his servant: The tree profiteth me nothing, and the roots thereof profit me nothing so long as it shall bring forth evil fruit.

36 Nevertheless, I know that the roots are good, and for mine own purpose I have preserved them; and because of their much strength they have hitherto brought forth, from the wild branches, good fruit.

37 But behold, the wild branches have grown and have overrun the roots thereof; and because that the wild branches have overcome the roots thereof it hath brought forth much evil fruit; and because that it hath brought forth so much evil fruit thou beholdest that it beginneth to perish; and it will soon become ripened, that it may be cast into the fire, except we should do something for it to preserve it.

38 And ... the Lord of the vineyard said unto his servant: Let us go down into the nethermost parts of the vineyard, and behold if the natural branches have also brought forth evil fruit.

39 And ... they went down into the nethermost parts of the vineyard. And ... they beheld that the fruit of the natural branches had become corrupt also; yea, the first and the second and also the last; and they had all become corrupt.[22]

40 And the wild fruit of the last had overcome that part of the tree which brought forth good fruit, even that the branch had withered away and died.

[23] Jacob 5:44. This refers to a previous migration of people, the Jaredites, who came to the New World centuries before Lehi and his family.
(Their story is told in the Book of Ether in the Book of Mormon, which
is not included in this volume.) Clearly, God is crushed that despite all
his efforts—including planting no less than two civilizations in the same
good ground—the people will not yield.

41 And … the Lord of the vineyard wept, and said unto the servant: What could I have done more for my vineyard?

42 Behold, I knew that all the fruit of the vineyard, save it were these, had become corrupted. And now these which have once brought forth good fruit have also become corrupted; and now all the trees of my vineyard are good for nothing save it be to be hewn down and cast into the fire.

43 And behold this last, whose branch hath withered away, I did plant in a good spot of ground; yea, even that which was choice unto me above all other parts of the land of my vineyard.

44 And thou beheldest that I also cut down that which cumbered this spot of ground, that I might plant this tree in the stead thereof.[23]

45 And thou beheldest that a part thereof brought forth good fruit, and a part thereof brought forth wild fruit; and because I plucked not the branches thereof and cast them into the fire, behold, they have overcome the good branch that it hath withered away.

46 And now, behold, notwithstanding all the care which we have taken of my vineyard, the trees thereof have become corrupted, that they bring forth no good fruit; and these I had hoped to preserve, to have laid up fruit thereof against the season, unto mine own self. But, behold, they have become like unto the wild olive-tree, and they are of no worth but to be hewn down and cast into the fire; and it grieveth me that I should lose them.

47 But what could I have done more in my vineyard? Have I slackened mine hand, that I have not nourished it, Nay, I have nourished it, and I have digged about it, and I have pruned it, and I have dunged it; and I have stretched forth mine hand almost all the day long, and the end draweth nigh. And it grieveth me that I should hew down all the trees of my vineyard, and cast them into the fire that they should be burned. Who is it that has corrupted my vineyard?

24 Jacob 5:49. LDS apostle Jeffrey R. Holland has written about what this verse teaches about the character of God. We see God's pain when, "after digging and dunging, watering and weeding, trimming, pruning, transplanting, and grafting, the great Lord of the vineyard throws down his spade and his pruning shears and weeps, crying out to any who would listen, 'What could I have done more for my vineyard?'"

48 And ... the servant said unto his master: Is it not the loftiness of thy vineyard—have not the branches thereof overcome the roots which are good? And because the branches have overcome the roots thereof, behold they grew faster than the strength of the roots, taking strength unto themselves. Behold, I say, is not this the cause that the trees of thy vineyard have become corrupted?

49 And ... the Lord of the vineyard said unto the servant: Let us go to and hew down the trees of the vineyard and cast them into the fire, that they shall not cumber the ground of my vineyard, for I have done all. What could I have done more for my vineyard?**24**

50 But, behold, the servant said unto the Lord of the vineyard: Spare it a little longer.

51 And the Lord said: Yea, I will spare it a little longer, for it grieveth me that I should lose the trees of my vineyard.

52 Wherefore, let us take of the branches of these which I have planted in the nethermost parts of my vineyard, and let us graft them into the tree from whence they came; and let us pluck from the tree those branches whose fruit is most bitter, and graft in the natural branches of the tree in the stead thereof.

53 And this will I do that the tree may not perish, that, perhaps, I may preserve unto myself the roots thereof for mine own purpose.

54 And, behold, the roots of the natural branches of the tree which I planted whithersoever I would are yet alive; wherefore, that I may preserve them also for mine own purpose, I will take of the branches of this tree, and I will graft them in unto them. Yea, I will graft in unto them the branches of their mother tree, that I may preserve the roots also unto mine own self, that when they shall be sufficiently strong perhaps they may bring forth good fruit unto me, and I may yet have glory in the fruit of my vineyard.

25 Jacob 5:56. This new grafting experiment—a last-ditch effort to save the trees—symbolizes the ultimate gathering of Israel from the ends of the earth. In the Mormon view, this means that scattered Israel will eventually convert to the gospel of Jesus Christ. Mormons believe this is already happening today as missionary work occurs in many nations.

26 Jacob 5:61. The other "servants" here symbolize all those select men and women whom the Lord will call throughout the world in the latter days—including, but not limited to, Joseph Smith and other prophets of the LDS Church.

55 And … they took from the natural tree which had become wild, and grafted in unto the natural trees, which also had become wild.

56 And they also took of the natural trees which had become wild, and grafted into their mother tree.**25**

57 And the Lord of the vineyard said unto the servant: Pluck not the wild branches from the trees, save it be those which are most bitter; and in them ye shall graft according to that which I have said.

58 And we will nourish again the trees of the vineyard, and we will trim up the branches thereof; and we will pluck from the trees those branches which are ripened, that must perish, and cast them into the fire.

59 And this I do that, perhaps, the roots thereof may take strength because of their goodness; and because of the change of the branches, that the good may overcome the evil.

60 And because that I have preserved the natural branches and the roots thereof, and that I have grafted in the natural branches again into their mother tree, and have preserved the roots of their mother tree, that, perhaps, the trees of my vineyard may bring forth again good fruit; and that I may have joy again in the fruit of my vineyard, and, perhaps, that I may rejoice exceedingly that I have preserved the roots and the branches of the first fruit—

61 Wherefore, go to, and call servants,**26** that we may labor diligently with our might in the vineyard, that we may prepare the way, that I may bring forth again the natural fruit, which natural fruit is good and the most precious above all other fruit.

62 Wherefore, let us go to and labor with our might this last time, for behold the end draweth nigh, and this is for the last time that I shall prune my vineyard.

27 │ Jacob 5:63. Lehi's descendants, among the last to be scattered, will be among the first to be gathered.

28 │ Jacob 5:66. The idea of the wicked being "hewn down" and "cast into the fire" is obviously offensive to many, but the allegory suggests here that this is the eventual fate of only those who stubbornly and actively resist God's every effort at reconciliation. Note that the verse begins with a restatement of how grieved God is that the wicked must be destroyed in the last days.

63 Graft in the branches; begin at the last that they may be first, and that the first may be last, and dig about the trees, both old and young, the first and the last; and the last and the first, that all may be nourished once again for the last time.**27**

64 Wherefore, dig about them, and prune them, and dung them once more, for the last time, for the end draweth nigh. And if it be so that these last grafts shall grow, and bring forth the natural fruit, then shall ye prepare the way for them, that they may grow.

65 And as they begin to grow ye shall clear away the branches which bring forth bitter fruit, according to the strength of the good and the size thereof; and ye shall not clear away the bad thereof all at once, lest the roots thereof should be too strong for the graft, and the graft thereof shall perish, and I lose the trees of my vineyard.

66 For it grieveth me that I should lose the trees of my vineyard; wherefore ye shall clear away the bad according as the good shall grow, that the root and the top may be equal in strength, until the good shall overcome the bad, and the bad be hewn down and cast into the fire, that they cumber not the ground of my vineyard; and thus will I sweep away the bad out of my vineyard.**28**

67 And the branches of the natural tree will I graft in again into the natural tree;

68 And the branches of the natural tree will I graft into the natural branches of the tree; and thus will I bring them together again, that they shall bring forth the natural fruit, and they shall be one.

69 And the bad shall be cast away, yea, even out of all the land of my vineyard; for behold, only this once will I prune my vineyard.

70 And ... the Lord of the vineyard sent his servant; and the servant went and did as the Lord had commanded him, and brought other servants; and they were few.

29 Jacob 5:71. Even in the last days, God will still try to nurture and nourish his people. Verses 71–75 describe a gradual process of purification and pruning in which God's people begin to thrive in his love and teachings, and the vineyard (the world) becomes free of corruption.

71 And the Lord of the vineyard said unto them: Go to, and labor in the vineyard, with your might. For behold, this is the last time that I shall nourish my vineyard; for the end is nigh at hand, and the season speedily cometh; and if ye labor with your might with me ye shall have joy in the fruit which I shall lay up unto myself against the time which will soon come.**29**

72 And ... the servants did go and labor with their mights; and the Lord of the vineyard labored also with them; and they did obey the commandments of the Lord of the vineyard in all things.

73 And there began to be the natural fruit again in the vineyard; and the natural branches began to grow and thrive exceedingly; and the wild branches began to be plucked off and to be cast away; and they did keep the root and the top thereof equal, according to the strength thereof.

74 And thus they labored, with all diligence, according to the commandments of the Lord of the vineyard, even until the bad had been cast away out of the vineyard, and the Lord had preserved unto himself that the trees had become again the natural fruit; and they became like unto one body; and the fruits were equal; and the Lord of the vineyard had preserved unto himself the natural fruit, which was most precious unto him from the beginning.

75 And ... when the Lord of the vineyard saw that his fruit was good, and that his vineyard was no more corrupt, he called up his servants, and said unto them: Behold, for this last time have we nourished my vineyard; and thou beholdest that I have done according to my will; and I have preserved the natural fruit, that it is good, even like as it was in the beginning. And blessed art thou; for because ye have been diligent in laboring with me in my vineyard, and have kept my commandments, and have brought unto me again the natural fruit,

30 Jacob 5:76–77. This refers to the *Millennium*, the eventual thousand-year reign of Christ upon the earth. During this time, Satan will be bound, but after the Millennium, his "evil fruit" (verse 77) will have one more opportunity to wreak havoc before God casts Satan off forever.

that my vineyard is no more corrupted, and the bad is cast away, behold ye shall have joy with me because of the fruit of my vineyard.

76 For behold, for a long time will I lay up of the fruit of my vineyard unto mine own self against the season, which speedily cometh; and for the last time have I nourished my vineyard, and pruned it, and dug about it, and dunged it; wherefore I will lay up unto mine own self of the fruit, for a long time, according to that which I have spoken.**30**

77 And when the time cometh that evil fruit shall again come into my vineyard, then will I cause the good and the bad to be gathered; and the good will I preserve unto myself, and the bad will I cast away into its own place. And then cometh the season and the end; and my vineyard will I cause to be burned with fire.

1 Mosiah 2:1. We have skipped ahead several hundred years to somewhere between 130 and 120 BCE. This sermon by the Nephite king, King Benjamin, is the longest and most comprehensive single sermon in the Book of Mormon; most of it is included here. The context for this message is that these are King Benjamin's final instructions to his people before his son Mosiah takes over the throne. He delivered this address outdoors at the Nephite temple.

4 □ The Book of Mosiah

King Benjamin's Sermon

Mosiah 2

1 And ... after Mosiah had done as his father had commanded him, and had made a proclamation throughout all the land, that the people gathered themselves together throughout all the land, that they might go up to the temple to hear the words which king Benjamin should speak unto them.**1**

. . . . .

8 And ... he began to speak to his people from the tower; and they could not all hear his words because of the greatness of the multitude; therefore he caused that the words which he spake should be written and sent forth among those that were not under the sound of his voice, that they might also receive his words.

9 And these are the words which he spake and caused to be written, saying: My brethren, all ye that have assembled yourselves together, you that can hear my words which I shall speak unto you this day; for I have not commanded you to come up hither to trifle with the words which I shall speak, but that you should hearken unto me, and open your ears that ye may hear, and your hearts that ye may understand, and your minds that the mysteries of God may be unfolded to your view.

10 I have not commanded you to come up hither that ye should fear me, or that ye should think that I of myself am more than a mortal man.

[2] Mosiah 2:11. The key theme of this chapter is service; in fact, Benjamin uses some form of the word *serve* fifteen times in chapter 2.

[3] Mosiah 2:14. Benjamin is an excellent example of a hands-on servant leader. One of the themes of the Book of Mormon is that righteous leaders labor with the people; they are not superior by nature to the people they serve. (This is why King Benjamin opens his speech with a reminder that he is prone to infirmities, just like his people, but has been chosen to serve them; see verse 11.) Because his people know him to be a model of integrity, they are inclined to listen to his long sermon, which includes some hard-hitting truths and numerous pleas for them to repent of their ways.

[4] Mosiah 2:17. This is one of the most frequently quoted passages in the Book of Mormon. The idea that serving other people is a way of serving God is a foundational aspect of Mormonism, which is lived out today in individual acts of service and also in institutional outreach programs like the LDS Humanitarian Relief Fund and the Church Welfare Program.

11 But I am like as yourselves, subject to all manner of infirmities in body and mind; yet I have been chosen by this people, and consecrated by my father, and was suffered by the hand of the Lord that I should be a ruler and a king over this people; and have been kept and preserved by his matchless power, to serve you with all the might, mind and strength which the Lord hath granted unto me.[2]

12 I say unto you that as I have been suffered to spend my days in your service, even up to this time, and have not sought gold nor silver nor any manner of riches of you;

13 Neither have I suffered that ye should be confined in dungeons, nor that ye should make slaves one of another, nor that ye should murder, or plunder, or steal, or commit adultery; nor even have I suffered that ye should commit any manner of wickedness, and have taught you that ye should keep the commandments of the Lord, in all things which he hath commanded you—

14 And even I, myself, have labored with mine own hands that I might serve you, and that ye should not be laden with taxes, and that there should nothing come upon you which was grievous to be borne— and of all these things which I have spoken, ye yourselves are witnesses this day.[3]

15 Yet, my brethren, I have not done these things that I might boast, neither do I tell these things that thereby I might accuse you; but I tell you these things that ye may know that I can answer a clear conscience before God this day.

16 Behold, I say unto you that because I said unto you that I had spent my days in your service, I do not desire to boast, for I have only been in the service of God.

17 And behold, I tell you these things that ye may learn wisdom; that ye may learn that when ye are in the service of your fellow beings ye are only in the service of your God.[4]

5   Mosiah 2:19. Benjamin presents service as the best way to thank God (here called the "heavenly King") for his blessings and care.

6   Mosiah 2:20–21. Benjamin teaches that even people whose souls are fully committed to God are "unprofitable servants." In Mormonism, no human being is considered capable of saving himself or herself; we must all lean on the merits of Christ and his atonement. Benjamin does not speak of Christ here (which he does further into his speech), but the connection is clear. As LDS president Joseph Fielding Smith taught, "we never could repay" Heavenly Father and Jesus Christ "no matter how hard we labor." The debt is simply too great.

18 Behold, ye have called me your king; and if I, whom ye call your king, do labor to serve you, then ought not ye to labor to serve one another?

19 And behold also, if I, whom ye call your king, who has spent his days in your service, and yet has been in the service of God, do merit any thanks from you, O how you ought to thank your heavenly King!**5**

20 I say unto you, my brethren, that if you should render all the thanks and praise which your whole soul has power to possess, to that God who has created you, and has kept and preserved you, and has caused that ye should rejoice, and has granted that ye should live in peace one with another—

21 I say unto you that if ye should serve him who has created you from the beginning, and is preserving you from day to day, by lending you breath, that ye may live and move and do according to your own will, and even supporting you from one moment to another—I say, if ye should serve him with all your whole souls yet ye would be unprofitable servants.**6**

22 And behold, all that he requires of you is to keep his commandments; and he has promised you that if ye would keep his commandments ye should prosper in the land; and he never doth vary from that which he hath said; therefore, if ye do keep his commandments he doth bless you and prosper you.

23 And now, in the first place, he hath created you, and granted unto you your lives, for which ye are indebted unto him.

24 And secondly, he doth require that ye should do as he hath commanded you; for which if ye do, he doth immediately bless you; and therefore he hath paid you. And ye are still indebted unto him, and are, and will be, forever and ever; therefore, of what have ye to boast?

7 | Mosiah 2:25. Benjamin calls his people to humility by reminding them that they are merely as dust. He brings the point home in the following verse by suggesting that he's about to return to dust himself, as he is old and death is imminent.

8 | Mosiah 2:36. Benjamin teaches that the stakes are far higher for people who have known and understood spiritual truth, and then chosen to reject it, than for those who never heard it at all.

25 And now I ask, can ye say aught of yourselves? I answer you, Nay. Ye cannot say that ye are even as much as the dust of the earth; yet ye were created of the dust of the earth; but behold, it belongeth to him who created you.**7**

26 And I, even I, whom ye call your king, am no better than ye yourselves are; for I am also of the dust. And ye behold that I am old, and am about to yield up this mortal frame to its mother earth.

27 Therefore, as I said unto you that I had served you, walking with a clear conscience before God, even so I at this time have caused that ye should assemble yourselves together, that I might be found blameless, and that your blood should not come upon me, when I shall stand to be judged of God of the things whereof he hath commanded me concerning you.

. . . . .

36 And now, I say unto you, my brethren, that after ye have known and have been taught all these things, if ye should transgress and go contrary to that which has been spoken, that ye do withdraw yourselves from the Spirit of the Lord,**8** that it may have no place in you to guide you in wisdom's paths that ye may be blessed, prospered, and preserved—

37 I say unto you, that the man that doeth this, the same cometh out in open rebellion against God; therefore he listeth to obey the evil spirit, and becometh an enemy to all righteousness; therefore, the Lord has no place in him, for he dwelleth not in unholy temples.

38 Therefore if that man repenteth not, and remaineth and dieth an enemy to God, the demands of divine justice do awaken his immortal soul to a lively sense of his own guilt, which doth cause him to shrink from the presence of the Lord, and doth fill his breast with guilt, and pain, and anguish, which is like an unquenchable fire, whose flame ascendeth up forever and ever.

9 | Mosiah 3:2. Benjamin reveals that he has been visited by an angel of God, who gave him an important message about the future.

10 | Mosiah 3:3. The wording here—"glad tidings of great joy"—is similar to the angelic message in Luke 2 in the New Testament, where angels impart "good tidings of great joy" to the shepherds. In both cases, the tidings referred to the coming birth of Christ.

11 | Mosiah 3:4. As with Lehi, Nephi, and other Book of Mormon figures, it's clear that Benjamin's vision was God's answer to his fervent prayer. The prayer comes first, not the revelation.

39 And now I say unto you, that mercy hath no claim on that man; therefore his final doom is to endure a never-ending torment.

40 O, all ye old men, and also ye young men, and you little children who can understand my words, for I have spoken plainly unto you that ye might understand, I pray that ye should awake to a remembrance of the awful situation of those that have fallen into transgression.

41 And moreover, I would desire that ye should consider on the blessed and happy state of those that keep the commandments of God. For behold, they are blessed in all things, both temporal and spiritual; and if they hold out faithful to the end they are received into heaven, that thereby they may dwell with God in a state of never-ending happiness. O remember, remember that these things are true; for the Lord God hath spoken it.

Mosiah 3

1 And again my brethren, I would call your attention, for I have somewhat more to speak unto you; for behold, I have things to tell you concerning that which is to come.

2 And the things which I shall tell you are made known unto me by an angel from God.[9] And he said unto me: Awake; and I awoke, and behold he stood before me.

3 And he said unto me: Awake, and hear the words which I shall tell thee; for behold, I am come to declare unto you the glad tidings of great joy.[10]

4 For the Lord hath heard thy prayers, and hath judged of thy righteousness, and hath sent me to declare unto thee that thou mayest rejoice; and that thou mayest declare unto thy people, that they may also be filled with joy.[11]

12 | Mosiah 3:8. After telling Benjamin many particulars about the coming Messiah, the angel reveals the Messiah's name: Jesus Christ. Also, Benjamin learns that Jesus's mother will be called Mary. Compare this to Nephi's vision, in which he glimpsed the mother and child but was not told the name of either (1 Nephi 11). Elsewhere in the Book of Mormon, we learn that God provides truth "line upon line, precept upon precept," as the people demonstrate readiness. (See also Isaiah 28.)

13 | Mosiah 3:11. Christ's sacrifice is not just for those who hear and believe his words, but for all those who died before his coming (including Benjamin and all his listeners, who must have been keen to hear these reassuring promises) and those who sinned without the gospel.

5 For behold, the time cometh, and is not far distant, that with power, the Lord Omnipotent who reigneth, who was, and is from all eternity to all eternity, shall come down from heaven among the children of men, and shall dwell in a tabernacle of clay, and shall go forth amongst men, working mighty miracles, such as healing the sick, raising the dead, causing the lame to walk, the blind to receive their sight, and the deaf to hear, and curing all manner of diseases.

6 And he shall cast out devils, or the evil spirits which dwell in the hearts of the children of men.

7 And lo, he shall suffer temptations, and pain of body, hunger, thirst, and fatigue, even more than man can suffer, except it be unto death; for behold, blood cometh from every pore, so great shall be his anguish for the wickedness and the abominations of his people.

8 And he shall be called Jesus Christ, the Son of God, the Father of heaven and earth, the Creator of all things from the beginning; and his mother shall be called Mary.[12]

9 And lo, he cometh unto his own, that salvation might come unto the children of men even through faith on his name; and even after all this they shall consider him a man, and say that he hath a devil, and shall scourge him, and shall crucify him.

10 And he shall rise the third day from the dead; and behold, he standeth to judge the world; and behold, all these things are done that a righteous judgment might come upon the children of men.

11 For behold, and also his blood atoneth for the sins of those who have fallen by the transgression of Adam, who have died not knowing the will of God concerning them, or who have ignorantly sinned.[13]

12 But wo, wo unto him who knoweth that he rebelleth against God! For salvation cometh to none such except it be through repentance and faith on the Lord Jesus Christ.

14 Mosiah 3:15. The law of Moses (the Ten Commandments and other ensuing *halakhot*—the laws arising from them) is important, but it is not enough to save people from their sins.

15 Mosiah 3:16–18. Mormons do not believe in *original sin*, the idea that the Fall of Adam and Eve is automatically passed from one generation to the next so that people are born in sin. In Mormon practice, children are not baptized until at least age eight, when they reach the *age of accountability* and are thought to be able to understand right from wrong. Here, Benjamin does not teach his hearers about baptism, but of salvation and sin in general. Since little children are not capable of fully knowing right from wrong, they are among the innocents who have "ignorantly sinned" (Mosiah 3:11) and are covered by the blood of Christ.

13 And the Lord God hath sent his holy prophets among all the children of men, to declare these things to every kindred, nation, and tongue, that thereby whosoever should believe that Christ should come, the same might receive remission of their sins, and rejoice with exceeding great joy, even as though he had already come among them.

14 Yet the Lord God saw that his people were a stiffnecked people, and he appointed unto them a law, even the law of Moses.

15 And many signs, and wonders, and types, and shadows showed he unto them, concerning his coming; and also holy prophets spake unto them concerning his coming; and yet they hardened their hearts, and understood not that the law of Moses availeth nothing except it were through the atonement of his blood.**14**

16 And even if it were possible that little children could sin they could not be saved; but I say unto you they are blessed; for behold, as in Adam, or by nature, they fall, even so the blood of Christ atoneth for their sins.

17 And moreover, I say unto you, that there shall be no other name given nor any other way nor means whereby salvation can come unto the children of men, only in and through the name of Christ, the Lord Omnipotent.

18 For behold he judgeth, and his judgment is just; and the infant perisheth not that dieth in his infancy; but men drink damnation to their own souls except they humble themselves and become as little children, and believe that salvation was, and is, and is to come, in and through the atoning blood of Christ, the Lord Omnipotent.**15**

19 For the natural man is an enemy to God, and has been from the fall of Adam, and will be, forever and ever, unless he yields to the enticings of the Holy Spirit, and putteth off the natural man and

16 Mosiah 3:19. Although Mormons reject the idea of original sin stemming from the Fall, they do believe that Adam and Eve by necessity brought physical death into the world. Here, Benjamin equates the "natural" man or woman with an unregenerated man or woman: These are people who have not been spiritually reborn in Christ.

becometh a saint through the atonement of Christ the Lord, and becometh as a child, submissive, meek, humble, patient, full of love, willing to submit to all things which the Lord seeth fit to inflict upon him, even as a child doth submit to his father.[16]

20 And moreover, I say unto you, that the time shall come when the knowledge of the Savior shall spread throughout every nation, kindred, tongue, and people.

21 And behold, when that time cometh, none shall be found blameless before God, except it be little children, only through repentance and faith on the name of the Lord God Omnipotent.

22 And even at this time, when thou shalt have taught thy people the things which the Lord thy God hath commanded thee, even then are they found no more blameless in the sight of God, only according to the words which I have spoken unto thee.

. . . . .

Mosiah 4

1 And ... when king Benjamin had made an end of speaking the words which had been delivered unto him by the angel of the Lord, he cast his eyes round about on the multitude, and behold they had fallen to the earth, for the fear of the Lord had come upon them.

2 And they had viewed themselves in their own carnal state, even less than the dust of the earth. And they all cried aloud with one voice, saying: O have mercy, and apply the atoning blood of Christ that we may receive forgiveness of our sins, and our hearts may be purified; for we believe in Jesus Christ, the Son of God, who created heaven and earth, and all things; who shall come down among the children of men.

17 Mosiah 4:2–3. Unlike other instances in the Book of Mormon and the Bible where prophets and other leaders call a people to repentance and they ignore it (at best) or kill the messenger (at worst), the Nephites respond with alacrity to King Benjamin's message, realizing their own humble state before God and asking forgiveness of their sins. This is a powerful example of collective contrition and repentance through prayer, all brought about because of the people's faith in the Savior who will come. In Mormonism, the first two principles of the gospel are faith in Jesus Christ, followed by repentance—two ideas that are amply illustrated in this passage.

3 And ... after they had spoken these words the Spirit of the Lord came upon them, and they were filled with joy, having received a remission of their sins, and having peace of conscience, because of the exceeding faith which they had in Jesus Christ who should come, according to the words which king Benjamin had spoken unto them.**17**

4 And king Benjamin again opened his mouth and began to speak unto them, saying: My friends and my brethren, my kindred and my people, I would again call your attention, that ye may hear and understand the remainder of my words which I shall speak unto you.

5 For behold, if the knowledge of the goodness of God at this time has awakened you to a sense of your nothingness, and your worthless and fallen state—

6 I say unto you, if ye have come to a knowledge of the goodness of God, and his matchless power, and his wisdom, and his patience, and his long-suffering towards the children of men; and also, the atonement which has been prepared from the foundation of the world, that thereby salvation might come to him that should put his trust in the Lord, and should be diligent in keeping his commandments, and continue in the faith even unto the end of his life, I mean the life of the mortal body—

7 I say, that this is the man who receiveth salvation, through the atonement which was prepared from the foundation of the world for all mankind, which ever were since the fall of Adam, or who are, or who ever shall be, even unto the end of the world.

8 And this is the means whereby salvation cometh. And there is none other salvation save this which hath been spoken of; neither are there any conditions whereby man can be saved except the conditions which I have told you.

18 Mosiah 4:10. For Mormons, as for many other Christians, repentance is not simply a one-time affair. On the Christian journey, people will invariably stumble and fall as they attempt to live the Lord's commandments. Repentance is necessary each time people sin or fall short of God's teachings—which is, of course, daily. As in any close relationship, the apology that is sincere repentance restores the bond between the sinner and the one sinned against.

19 Mosiah 4:11. Note the use of "remember" and "retain," words that are picked up again in Mosiah 5:12. Benjamin wants his listeners to always remember their own humble state compared to God's greatness. In the next verse, he ties this remembrance to the remission of sins, which is a startling connection. In other words, unless people remember their "own nothingness," they risk losing their connection with God and possibly also the forgiveness (remission) they once obtained through genuine repentance.

9 Believe in God; believe that he is, and that he created all things, both in heaven and in earth; believe that he has all wisdom, and all power, both in heaven and in earth; believe that man doth not comprehend all the things which the Lord can comprehend.

10 And again, believe that ye must repent of your sins and forsake them, and humble yourselves before God; and ask in sincerity of heart that he would forgive you; and now, if you believe all these things see that ye do them.**18**

11 And again I say unto you as I have said before, that as ye have come to the knowledge of the glory of God, or if ye have known of his goodness and have tasted of his love, and have received a remission of your sins, which causeth such exceeding great joy in your souls, even so I would that ye should remember, and always retain in remembrance,**19** the greatness of God, and your own nothingness, and his goodness and long-suffering towards you, unworthy creatures, and humble yourselves even in the depths of humility, calling on the name of the Lord daily, and standing steadfastly in the faith of that which is to come, which was spoken by the mouth of the angel.

12 And behold, I say unto you that if ye do this ye shall always rejoice, and be filled with the love of God, and always retain a remission of your sins; and ye shall grow in the knowledge of the glory of him that created you, or in the knowledge of that which is just and true.

13 And ye will not have a mind to injure one another, but to live peaceably, and to render to every man according to that which is his due.

14 And ye will not suffer your children that they go hungry, or naked; neither will ye suffer that they transgress the laws of God, and fight and quarrel one with another, and serve the devil, who is the master of sin, or who is the evil spirit which hath been spoken of by our fathers, he being an enemy to all righteousness.

20 Mosiah 4:17. Christians are expected not just to be generous to the poor, but to refrain from making judgments about the poor. They cannot "stay their hand" (abstain from giving) just because they think that the recipient is poor for a reason—that she doesn't work hard enough, or he has brought this misery upon himself. In other words, the commandment to give generously and take care of the poor is unmitigated by circumstance; we are told to give, period.

21 Mosiah 4:19. Again, King Benjamin comes back to the theme of humility. Here, he connects people's stinginess and desire to withhold charity from the dependent poor to our own all-too-human state of dependence.

22 Mosiah 4:21. Benjamin reminds his listeners that they are dependent upon God for everything—and that God has been abundantly generous with them, withholding nothing. God's liberal, open-handed nature is a model for all people.

15 But ye will teach them to walk in the ways of truth and soberness; ye will teach them to love one another, and to serve one another.

16 And also, ye yourselves will succor those that stand in need of your succor; ye will administer of your substance unto him that standeth in need; and ye will not suffer that the beggar putteth up his petition to you in vain, and turn him out to perish.

17 Perhaps thou shalt say: The man has brought upon himself his misery;[20] therefore I will stay my hand, and will not give unto him of my food, nor impart unto him of my substance that he may not suffer, for his punishments are just—

18 But I say unto you, O man, whosoever doeth this the same hath great cause to repent; and except he repenteth of that which he hath done he perisheth forever, and hath no interest in the kingdom of God.

19 For behold, are we not all beggars? Do we not all depend upon the same Being, even God, for all the substance which we have, for both food and raiment, and for gold, and for silver, and for all the riches which we have of every kind?[21]

20 And behold, even at this time, ye have been calling on his name, and begging for a remission of your sins. And has he suffered that ye have begged in vain? Nay; he has poured out his Spirit upon you, and has caused that your hearts should be filled with joy, and has caused that your mouths should be stopped that ye could not find utterance, so exceeding great was your joy.

21 And now, if God, who has created you, on whom you are dependent for your lives and for all that ye have and are, doth grant unto you whatsoever ye ask that is right, in faith, believing that ye shall receive, O then, how ye ought to impart of the substance that ye have one to another.[22]

23 Mosiah 4:26. Benjamin clarifies the reasons why people should take care of the poor. It's not just because it's a "nice" thing to do; it's necessary if they wish to "retain a remission" of their sins. Essentially, Benjamin wants his listeners to put their faith into action. It's not enough to repent and be forgiven of sins; Christ's followers have to then put divine love into action by living lives of service. This is part of what it means to "walk guiltless" before God.

24 Mosiah 4:27. In dealing with poverty—which can seem overwhelming, as the needs of the poor are so vast—Benjamin cautions that people don't need to "run faster" than their strength allows. They will never be able to take care of all people's needs at all times. However, it is essential that they act generously to do what they can.

22 And if ye judge the man who putteth up his petition to you for your substance that he perish not, and condemn him, how much more just will be your condemnation for withholding your substance, which doth not belong to you but to God, to whom also your life belongeth; and yet ye put up no petition, nor repent of the thing which thou hast done.

23 I say unto you, wo be unto that man, for his substance shall perish with him; and now, I say these things unto those who are rich as pertaining to the things of this world.

24 And again, I say unto the poor, ye who have not and yet have sufficient, that ye remain from day to day; I mean all you who deny the beggar, because ye have not; I would that ye say in your hearts that: I give not because I have not, but if I had I would give.

25 And now, if ye say this in your hearts ye remain guiltless, otherwise ye are condemned; and your condemnation is just for ye covet that which ye have not received.

26 And now, for the sake of these things which I have spoken unto you—that is, for the sake of retaining a remission of your sins from day to day, that ye may walk guiltless before God—I would that ye should impart of your substance to the poor, every man according to that which he hath, such as feeding the hungry, clothing the naked, visiting the sick and administering to their relief, both spiritually and temporally, according to their wants.[23]

27 And see that all these things are done in wisdom and order; for it is not requisite that a man should run faster than he has strength. And again, it is expedient that he should be diligent, that thereby he might win the prize; therefore, all things must be done in order.[24]

28 And I would that ye should remember, that whosoever among you borroweth of his neighbor should return the thing that he

25   Mosiah 4:30. This verse reiterates a theme that is explored elsewhere in Christian scripture: people will be judged not just by their deeds but also by their innermost thoughts. This points to the fact that our thoughts shape who we are spiritually; God is interested in our interior lives as well as our outward actions. As Proverbs 23:7 suggests, a person *becomes* what he or she thinks. Salvation is not simply behavioral, but fully ontological.

26   Mosiah 5:2. The "mighty change" discussed here is religious conversion.

borroweth, according as he doth agree, or else thou shalt commit sin; and perhaps thou shalt cause thy neighbor to commit sin also.

29 And finally, I cannot tell you all the things whereby ye may commit sin; for there are divers ways and means, even so many that I cannot number them.

30 But this much I can tell you, that if ye do not watch yourselves, and your thoughts, and your words, and your deeds, and observe the commandments of God, and continue in the faith of what ye have heard concerning the coming of our Lord, even unto the end of your lives, ye must perish. And now, O man, remember, and perish not.[25]

Mosiah 5

1 And ... when king Benjamin had thus spoken to his people, he sent among them, desiring to know of his people if they believed the words which he had spoken unto them.

2 And they all cried with one voice, saying: Yea, we believe all the words which thou hast spoken unto us; and also, we know of their surety and truth, because of the Spirit of the Lord Omnipotent, which has wrought a mighty change[26] in us, or in our hearts, that we have no more disposition to do evil, but to do good continually.

3 And we, ourselves, also, through the infinite goodness of God, and the manifestations of his Spirit, have great views of that which is to come; and were it expedient, we could prophesy of all things.

4 And it is the faith which we have had on the things which our king has spoken unto us that has brought us to this great knowledge, whereby we do rejoice with such exceeding great joy.

5 And we are willing to enter into a covenant with our God to do his will, and to be obedient to his commandments in all things that he

27 Mosiah 5:7. After the people enter into their covenant with God and pledge their obedience, they receive the name that Benjamin had hinted at earlier in Mosiah 1:11: "I shall give this people a name, that thereby they may be distinguished above all the people which the Lord God hath brought out of the land of Jerusalem." The name can only be blotted out if the people transgress. The name, we learn in Mosiah 5:7, is "the children of Christ."

shall command us, all the remainder of our days, that we may not bring upon ourselves a never-ending torment, as has been spoken by the angel, that we may not drink out of the cup of the wrath of God.

6 And now, these are the words which king Benjamin desired of them; and therefore he said unto them: Ye have spoken the words that I desired; and the covenant which ye have made is a righteous covenant.

7 And now, because of the covenant which ye have made ye shall be called the children of Christ,**27** his sons, and his daughters; for behold, this day he hath spiritually begotten you; for ye say that your hearts are changed through faith on his name; therefore, ye are born of him and have become his sons and his daughters.

8 And under this head ye are made free, and there is no other head whereby ye can be made free. There is no other name given whereby salvation cometh; therefore, I would that ye should take upon you the name of Christ, all you that have entered into the covenant with God that ye should be obedient unto the end of your lives.

9 And it shall come to pass that whosoever doeth this shall be found at the right hand of God, for he shall know the name by which he is called; for he shall be called by the name of Christ.

10 And now it shall come to pass, that whosoever shall not take upon him the name of Christ must be called by some other name; therefore, he findeth himself on the left hand of God.

11 And I would that ye should remember also, that this is the name that I said I should give unto you that never should be blotted out, except it be through transgression; therefore, take heed that ye do not transgress, that the name be not blotted out of your hearts.

12 I say unto you, I would that ye should remember to retain the name written always in your hearts, that ye are not found on the left hand

28 | Mosiah 5:15. Benjamin's final prayer for his people is a beautiful summation of his wish that they be "steadfast" and "immovable" followers of Christ.

of God, but that ye hear and know the voice by which ye shall be called, and also, the name by which he shall call you.

. . . . .

15 Therefore, I would that ye should be steadfast and immovable, always abounding in good works, that Christ, the Lord God Omnipotent, may seal you his, that you may be brought to heaven, that ye may have everlasting salvation and eternal life, through the wisdom, and power, and justice, and mercy of him who created all things, in heaven and in earth, who is God above all. Amen.[28]

1 Alma 5:1. We now skip ahead a couple of generations to around 83 BCE. Alma, the hero of this section of the Book of Mormon, has just resigned from being the chief judge of the Nephite people, but he has retained the title of high priest in order to go on a preaching tour of Nephite communities and try to convert them to the gospel. Alma realizes that the most important task he can undertake is to devote himself wholly to the goal of the spiritual welfare of his people. The Nephites, many of whom have been taught the true religion, nevertheless have succumbed to pride and wickedness, so the need for missionary work is great. Alma goes to the city of Zarahemla to preach this message.

Note that this Alma is also called "Alma the Younger" because his father shared the same name. (One of the most confusing aspects of following the Book of Mormon is the prevalence of the same name popping up in generations of Lehi's descendants. Other popular names include Nephi, Helaman, Lehi, and Moroni.)

2 Alma 5:2–4. Alma begins his teachings with a reminder of the many ways God has been faithful to the Nephites. Note that King Noah, mentioned in verse 4, is not the same Noah readers may be familiar with from the Old Testament/Hebrew Bible. In contrast to that Noah, who endured censure in order to follow God's commandments and saved a righteous remnant from the Great Flood, the Book of Mormon's King Noah nearly brought his small colony of Nephites to ruin through "whoredoms," corrupt priests, excessive taxation, and self-indulgence. He was eventually burned to death by his own people.

5 □ The Book of Alma

Repentance and Spiritual Rebirth

Alma 5

1 Now ... Alma[1] began to deliver the word of God unto the people, first in the land of Zarahemla, and from thence throughout all the land.

2 And these are the words which he spake to the people in the church which was established in the city of Zarahemla, according to his own record, saying:

3 I, Alma, having been consecrated by my father, Alma, to be a high priest over the church of God, he having power and authority from God to do these things, behold, I say unto you that he began to establish a church in the land which was in the borders of Nephi; yea, the land which was called the land of Mormon; yea, and he did baptize his brethren in the waters of Mormon.

4 And behold, I say unto you, they were delivered out of the hands of the people of king Noah,[2] by the mercy and power of God.

3 | Alma 5:5. There is an important pronoun change in verse 5. Alma begins by stating that "they" (the ancestors of his Nephite audience) were in captivity, but then turns the tables by using the first person plural pronoun "we." His little history lesson is not academic: It is designed to help the Nephites understand how they, like their ancestors, have been established by God but have strayed from the truth.

4 | Alma 5:6. Alma employs the language of King Benjamin's sermon to call the Nephites to task for turning away from the covenants their parents and grandparents once made. The query "have you sufficiently retained in remembrance" is repeated three times. Also, there is an important repetition of the theme of captivity here. Alma seems to be recalling his own dramatic conversion some years earlier, when an angel of the Lord used the same language ("remember the captivity of thy fathers") to bring *him* to humility and repentance (Mosiah 27:16). As Alma was once taught, so he now teaches others.

5 | Alma 5:10. Faith is what saves people and offers them freedom from the "bands of death" and the "chains of hell."

6 | Alma 5:11. Here, Alma the Younger recalls the example of his father, whom we might call "Alma senior," who was converted to the truth when he was, ironically enough, serving in the court of King Noah: he learned of faith and righteousness under the wicked ruler's own roof. A prophet named Abinadi came to Noah's kingdom to teach the gospel, and although he suffered a fate of execution, he did win a few souls before his death. These included his most important convert, Alma senior.

5 And behold, after that, they were brought into bondage by the hands of the Lamanites in the wilderness; yea, I say unto you, they were in captivity, and again the Lord did deliver them out of bondage by the power of his word; and we[3] were brought into this land, and here we began to establish the church of God throughout this land also.

6 And now behold, I say unto you, my brethren, you that belong to this church, have you sufficiently retained in remembrance[4] the captivity of your fathers? Yea, and have you sufficiently retained in remembrance his mercy and long-suffering towards them? And moreover, have ye sufficiently retained in remembrance that he has delivered their souls from hell?

7 Behold, he changed their hearts; yea, he awakened them out of a deep sleep, and they awoke unto God. Behold, they were in the midst of darkness; nevertheless, their souls were illuminated by the light of the everlasting word; yea, they were encircled about by the bands of death, and the chains of hell, and an everlasting destruction did await them.

8 And now I ask of you, my brethren, were they destroyed? Behold, I say unto you, Nay, they were not.

9 And again I ask, were the bands of death broken, and the chains of hell which encircled them about, were they loosed? I say unto you, Yea, they were loosed, and their souls did expand, and they did sing redeeming love. And I say unto you that they are saved.

10 And now I ask of you on what conditions are they saved? Yea, what grounds had they to hope for salvation? What is the cause of their being loosed from the bands of death, yea, and also the chains of hell?[5]

11 Behold, I can tell you—did not my father Alma[6] believe in the words which were delivered by the mouth of Abinadi? And was he not a

7 | Alma 5:14. Alma asks the members of the church the critical question: Are they truly converted? Without the "mighty change" that comes with knowing God, their membership in an organization or affiliation with a church will not be very meaningful. The real test is whether people are acting in a Christ-like way ("Have ye received his image in your countenances?") and transforming their lives to conform with Christ's teachings. To understand this, it's helpful to return to an older definition of "countenance," which means not just one's face or likeness, but also one's demeanor, bearing, and even behavior.

8 | Alma 5:26. Alma gets right to the heart of things when he essentially asks his listeners to recall what it felt like to become converted and "sing the song of redeeming love." If they felt that way once upon a time, he implores, can they feel so now?

holy prophet? Did he not speak the words of God, and my father Alma believe them?

12 And according to his faith there was a mighty change wrought in his heart. Behold I say unto you that this is all true.

13 And behold, he preached the word unto your fathers, and a mighty change was also wrought in their hearts, and they humbled themselves and put their trust in the true and living God. And behold, they were faithful until the end; therefore they were saved.

14 And now behold, I ask of you, my brethren of the church, have ye spiritually been born of God?[7] Have ye received his image in your countenances? Have ye experienced this mighty change in your hearts?

15 Do ye exercise faith in the redemption of him who created you? Do you look forward with an eye of faith, and view this mortal body raised in immortality, and this corruption raised in incorruption, to stand before God to be judged according to the deeds which have been done in the mortal body?

16 I say unto you, can you imagine to yourselves that ye hear the voice of the Lord, saying unto you, in that day: Come unto me ye blessed, for behold, your works have been the works of righteousness upon the face of the earth?

. . . . .

26 And now behold, I say unto you, my brethren, if ye have experienced a change of heart, and if ye have felt to sing the song of redeeming love, I would ask, can ye feel so now?[8]

27 Have ye walked, keeping yourselves blameless before God? Could ye say, if ye were called to die at this time, within yourselves, that ye have been sufficiently humble? That your garments have been

9 Alma 5:27–30. Alma provides his listeners (and us, as readers) with a kind of spiritual checklist of ways to discern true conversion. People who've experienced a mighty change of heart try to keep themselves blameless by being humble (verse 28), avoiding jealousy (verse 29), and refraining from mockery of others (verse 30). They feel that if they were to die today, they would die "sufficiently humble" in the knowledge that Christ has redeemed them from their sins (verse 27).

10 Alma 5:40–42. Again, the Book of Mormon emphasizes that true followers of Christ will be known by their fruits, which are good works. The basic dualism that is posited here is actually tempered by some of the real situations present in the Book of Mormon (and in life), where sometimes good and evil are not always so easy to define.

cleansed and made white through the blood of Christ, who will come to redeem his people from their sins?

28 Behold, are ye stripped of pride? I say unto you, if ye are not ye are not prepared to meet God. Behold ye must prepare quickly; for the kingdom of heaven is soon at hand, and such an one hath not eternal life.

29 Behold, I say, is there one among you who is not stripped of envy? I say unto you that such an one is not prepared; and I would that he should prepare quickly, for the hour is close at hand, and he knoweth not when the time shall come; for such an one is not found guiltless.

30 And again I say unto you, is there one among you that doth make a mock of his brother, or that heapeth upon him persecutions?**9**

31 Wo unto such an one, for he is not prepared, and the time is at hand that he must repent or he cannot be saved!

. . . . .

40 For I say unto you that whatsoever is good cometh from God, and whatsoever is evil cometh from the devil.

41 Therefore, if a man bringeth forth good works he hearkeneth unto the voice of the good shepherd, and he doth follow him; but whosoever bringeth forth evil works, the same becometh a child of the devil, for he hearkeneth unto his voice, and doth follow him.**10**

42 And whosoever doeth this must receive his wages of him; therefore, for his wages he receiveth death, as to things pertaining unto righteousness, being dead unto all good works.

. . . . .

53 And now my beloved brethren, I say unto you, can ye withstand these sayings; yea, can ye lay aside these things, and trample the Holy One under your feet; yea, can ye be puffed up in the pride of

11 Alma 5:53–55. Winding down his sermon, Alma recapitulates a few
of the key points as he beseeches his audience to start living the gospel.
How can they be believers in Christ, he asks, when they are so "puffed
up" with pride that they set their hearts on the things of this world?
How can they claim to be church members, when they continue to
imagine that they are superior to other people and persist in ignoring
the needs of the poor?

12 Alma 5:58. This is the only time that the term *book of life* appears
in the Book of Mormon. The Old Testament/Hebrew Bible and several
places in the New Testament (most heavily in the Book of Revelation)
suggest that there is a record kept in heaven of human righteousness.
In the Doctrine and Covenants (another book of Mormon scripture),
it is suggested that the dead will be judged according to the record that
is contained in the Book of Life, an idea that has consonance with
Judaism.

your hearts; yea, will ye still persist in the wearing of costly apparel and setting your hearts upon the vain things of the world, upon your riches?**11**

54 Yea, will ye persist in supposing that ye are better one than another; yea, will ye persist in the persecution of your brethren, who humble themselves and do walk after the holy order of God, wherewith they have been brought into this church, having been sanctified by the Holy Spirit, and they do bring forth works which are meet for repentance—

55 Yea, and will you persist in turning your backs upon the poor, and the needy, and in withholding your substance from them?

56 And finally, all ye that will persist in your wickedness, I say unto you that these are they who shall be hewn down and cast into the fire except they speedily repent.

57 And now I say unto you, all you that are desirous to follow the voice of the good shepherd, come ye out from the wicked, and be ye separate, and touch not their unclean things; and behold, their names shall be blotted out, that the names of the wicked shall not be numbered among the names of the righteous, that the word of God may be fulfilled, which saith: The names of the wicked shall not be mingled with the names of my people;

58 For the names of the righteous shall be written in the book of life,**12** and unto them will I grant an inheritance at my right hand. And now, my brethren, what have ye to say against this? I say unto you, if ye speak against it, it matters not, for the word of God must be fulfilled.

59 For what shepherd is there among you having many sheep doth not watch over them, that the wolves enter not and devour his flock? And behold, if a wolf enter his flock doth he not drive him out? Yea, and at the last, if he can, he will destroy him.

13 Alma 12. The context for this section is important: whereas in chapter 5 we saw Alma preaching to an audience of people in the city of Zarahemla who were primarily members of "the Church" (i.e., baptized into Nephite religion) but had not been living up to its precepts, here he is in the city of Ammonihah—a city that may have been founded explicitly by people who wanted to have nothing to do with Nephite religion. Alma has already been there to preach, and it didn't end well; he might not have tried returning had he not been directly instructed by an angel to do so (Alma 8:14–16). On his second visit, he finds a kindred spirit in a righteous Ammonihah resident named Amulek, who agrees to help him in his missionary work. In Alma 12 and 13, Alma offers some of the Book of Mormon's most important teachings on the judgment day, the purpose of life, and the plan of salvation.

14 Alma 12:14. The Book of Mormon teaches that we won't just be judged by our works, but also by our words and even our thoughts. Because no person can hope to attain a perfectly righteous synthesis of thoughts and deeds, we will all have cause to tremble when one day we come face-to-face with God.

60 And now I say unto you that the good shepherd doth call after you; and if you will hearken unto his voice he will bring you into his fold, and ye are his sheep; and he commandeth you that ye suffer no ravenous wolf to enter among you, that ye may not be destroyed.

61 And now I, Alma, do command you in the language of him who hath commanded me, that ye observe to do the words which I have spoken unto you.

62 I speak by way of command unto you that belong to the church; and unto those who do not belong to the church I speak by way of invitation, saying: Come and be baptized unto repentance, that ye also may be partakers of the fruit of the tree of life.

. . . . .

Death and Judgment

Alma 12¹³

. . . . .

13 Then if our hearts have been hardened, yea, if we have hardened our hearts against the word, insomuch that it has not been found in us, then will our state be awful, for then we shall be condemned.

14 For our words will condemn us, yea, all our works will condemn us; we shall not be found spotless; and our thoughts will also condemn us; and in this awful state we shall not dare to look up to our God; and we would fain be glad if we could command the rocks and the mountains to fall upon us to hide us from his presence.**14**

15 But this cannot be; we must come forth and stand before him in his glory, and in his power, and in his might, majesty, and dominion, and acknowledge to our everlasting shame that all his judgments are just;

15 Alma 12:15. Although human beings have no cause to stand upright before God in boasting of their *own* righteousness, they trust in his mercy as well as his justice.

16 Alma 12:16. Because the fall of Adam and Eve brought physical death into the world, all human beings are subject to the power of "the first death," which is the natural physical passing that is part and parcel of mortality. However, physical death is not the end of the soul. We can decide through the exercise of our agency whether we will experience eternal life or a second spiritual death. Here, Alma teaches that those individuals who die before they have repented of their sins are dead "as to things pertaining unto righteousness."

17 John Taylor, who was the third president and prophet of the LDS Church, spoke about Satan's role and power to tempt humanity: "Who is Satan? A being powerful, energetic, deceptive, insinuating; and yet necessary…. He is a being of God's own make, under his control, subject to his will, cast out of heaven for rebellion; and when his services can be dispensed with, an angel will cast him into the bottomless pit."

18 Alma 12:24. To Mormons, the great purpose of life is to "prepare to meet God," which is accomplished through exercising faith in Jesus Christ and in following God's commandments. This life is considered a "probationary state," or testing ground, to prepare individuals for an exalted heavenly afterlife with God. In Mormon theology, that state of permanent paradise occurs after souls have congregated in the spirit world and then been judged at the day of resurrection.

that he is just in all his works, and that he is merciful unto the children of men, and that he has all power to save every man that believeth on his name and bringeth forth fruit meet for repentance.**15**

16 And now behold, I say unto you then cometh a death, even a second death,**16** which is a spiritual death; then is a time that whosoever dieth in his sins, as to a temporal death, shall also die a spiritual death; yea, he shall die as to things pertaining unto righteousness.

17 Then is the time when their torments shall be as a lake of fire and brimstone, whose flame ascendeth up forever and ever; and then is the time that they shall be chained down to an everlasting destruction, according to the power and captivity of Satan, he having subjected them according to his will.**17**

18 Then, I say unto you, they shall be as though there had been no redemption made; for they cannot be redeemed according to God's justice; and they cannot die, seeing there is no more corruption.

. . . . .

24 And we see that death comes upon mankind, yea, the death which has been spoken of by Amulek, which is the temporal death; nevertheless there was a space granted unto man in which he might repent; therefore this life became a probationary state;**18** a time to prepare to meet God; a time to prepare for that endless state which has been spoken of by us, which is after the resurrection of the dead.

25 Now, if it had not been for the plan of redemption, which was laid from the foundation of the world, there could have been no resurrection of the dead; but there was a plan of redemption laid, which shall bring to pass the resurrection of the dead, of which has been spoken.

26 And now behold, if it were possible that our first parents could have gone forth and partaken of the tree of life they would have been

19 Alma 12:26. Alma is referring here to Adam and Eve's valiant decision to eat the fruit offered to them in the Garden of Eden. Without it, they would have been "forever miserable" because they would have had no opportunity to improve their stagnant situation and childlike state (2 Nephi 2:21). In Mormonism, spiritual progress is paramount, both in this life (the preparatory state Alma speaks of) and in the life to come.

20 Alma 12:34. What God requires is that human beings ask forgiveness for their sins and keep their hearts open to his mercy.

21 Alma 32:17. This extended treatise on faith and knowledge is widely considered one of the most beautiful passages of the Book of Mormon. Eugene England, the late Mormon scholar, considered it one of the most marvelous and hopeful statements about faith in all of scripture. In essence, Alma builds the case that faith is necessary for spiritual growth—an argument that has clear equivalents in the Bible and elsewhere. If people had all the signs and miracles that they crave, they'd never have to exercise their faith. (And in many cases, people who claim that they'd become believers simply if they experienced a miracle are fooling themselves. In the Book of Mormon, the example of Laman and Lemuel, who were privy to all kinds of signs and wonders but stubbornly hardened their hearts, reminds us that lasting faith does not result from merely being a passive witness to supernatural events.) As we'll see, Alma takes the faith argument one step further, however, arguing that faith is but a precursor to sure knowledge; in fact, he even suggests that in some ways faith may be superior to knowledge.

forever miserable,**19** having no preparatory state; and thus the plan of redemption would have been frustrated, and the word of God would have been void, taking none effect.

27 But behold, it was not so; but it was appointed unto men that they must die; and after death, they must come to judgment, even that same judgment of which we have spoken, which is the end.

. . . . .

34 Therefore, whosoever repenteth, and hardeneth not his heart,**20** he shall have claim on mercy through mine Only Begotten Son, unto a remission of his sins; and these shall enter into my rest.

35 And whosoever will harden his heart and will do iniquity, behold, I swear in my wrath that he shall not enter into my rest.

. . . . .

On Faith and Knowledge

Alma 32

. . . . .

17 Yea, there are many who do say: If thou wilt show unto us a sign from heaven, then we shall know of a surety; then we shall believe.**21**

18 Now I ask, is this faith? Behold, I say unto you, Nay; for if a man knoweth a thing he hath no cause to believe, for he knoweth it.

(continued on page 155)

22 | Alma 32:19. Interestingly, Alma opens his discussion of faith and knowledge by mentioning again what has become a common theme in the Book of Mormon: that people will be held responsible for the level of knowledge they have received or acquired regarding spiritual things. In other words, the Lord doesn't simply award people with miracles because those people would then be held accountable for a level of spiritual knowledge they have not genuinely attained through exercising faith. In mercy and kindness, God doesn't burden human beings with more spiritual knowledge than they can bear, preferring to lead them gently and slowly through the stages of faith to a sure knowledge. (See also verse 22.) Brigham Young University professor Rodney Turner says that God has "ordained that faith must precede certitude so that, in the very process of exercising faith, the individual develops the spiritual maturity needed to possess divine knowledge in righteousness."

23 | Alma 32:21. Faith, which is to "hope for things which are not seen, which are true," is fundamentally different than a perfect knowledge. It is a stage of *hoping* for knowledge and truth, and of stepping out of one's comfort zone to test the truth of something.

24 | Alma 32:24. The context for this sermon is that Alma is speaking to a group of poor, despised Zoramite people. The Zoramites were an apostate, offshoot group of the Nephites who had perverted Nephite religion and declared that belief in Christ was foolish. (To be fair, Christ's birth was still a future event, so they were rejecting something they had not seen and which therefore required the exercise of faith.) In their pride, the Zoramites also banished the poor from worshiping in their synagogues, and it is these same downtrodden individuals who were receptive to Alma's message. It is likely that he was the first priest or person of spiritual stature to care for them at all, and they humbly responded to his teachings.

19 And now, how much more cursed is he that knoweth the will of God and doeth it not, than he that only believeth, or only hath cause to believe, and falleth into transgression?**22**

20 Now of this thing ye must judge. Behold, I say unto you, that it is on the one hand even as it is on the other; and it shall be unto every man according to his work.

21 And now as I said concerning faith—faith is not to have a perfect knowledge of things; therefore if ye have faith ye hope for things which are not seen, which are true.**23**

22 And now, behold, I say unto you, and I would that ye should remember, that God is merciful unto all who believe on his name; therefore he desireth, in the first place, that ye should believe, yea, even on his word.

23 And now, he imparteth his word by angels unto men, yea, not only men but women also. Now this is not all; little children do have words given unto them many times which confound the wise and the learned.

24 And now, my beloved brethren, as ye have desired to know of me what ye shall do because ye are afflicted and cast out**24**—now I do not desire that ye should suppose that I mean to judge you only according to that which is true—

25 For I do not mean that ye all of you have been compelled to humble yourselves; for I verily believe that there are some among you who would humble themselves, let them be in whatsoever circumstances they might.

(continued on page 157)

25 Alma 32:26. Alma's words have to be tested and put into practice before listeners will fully understand their truth.

26 Alma 32:27. A "particle of faith" is all that's needed to begin Alma's experiment. This particle comes into being merely because of a sincere *desire* to believe; the desire begins the whole process of faith, testing, and knowledge.

27 Alma 32:28. Alma calls upon the principle, which has been elucidated elsewhere in the Book of Mormon, that a good seed will necessarily bear good fruit. In his listeners' case, a person can know the truth of a spiritual matter (such as the reality of Christ, which the proud Zoramites had denied) by what happens when it's planted. If the seed bears fruit after nourishment—in this case, by filling the individual with the swelling love of the Holy Spirit after he or she prays to know if it is worthwhile to believe in Christ—then the person can know the seed was good (i.e., that the doctrine is true). The experimenter can ask three foundational questions on any spiritual issue or question: Does this belief, once put into practice, enlarge my soul? Does it enlighten my understanding? Is it beginning to taste "delicious" enough that I desire more?

28 Alma 32:29–30. Alma cautions that this is not the end of the process. Faith has been exercised and strengthened, but the individual doesn't possess a perfect knowledge yet. Note that the 1981 edition of verse 30 contains an additional sentence that was restored from the earliest manuscript of the Book of Mormon: "And now behold, will not this strengthen your faith? Yea, it will strengthen your faith: for ye will say I know that this is a good seed; for behold it sprouteth and beginneth to grow."

26 Now, as I said concerning faith—that it was not a perfect knowledge—even so it is with my words. Ye cannot know of their surety at first, unto perfection, any more than faith is a perfect knowledge.**25**

27 But behold, if ye will awake and arouse your faculties, even to an experiment upon my words, and exercise a particle of faith,**26** yea, even if ye can no more than desire to believe, let this desire work in you, even until ye believe in a manner that ye can give place for a portion of my words.

28 Now, we will compare the word unto a seed. Now, if ye give place, that a seed may be planted in your heart, behold, if it be a true seed, or a good seed, if ye do not cast it out by your unbelief, that ye will resist the Spirit of the Lord, behold, it will begin to swell within your breasts; and when you feel these swelling motions, ye will begin to say within yourselves—It must needs be that this is a good seed, or that the word is good, for it beginneth to enlarge my soul; yea, it beginneth to enlighten my understanding, yea, it beginneth to be delicious to me.**27**

29 Now behold, would not this increase your faith? I say unto you, Yea; nevertheless it hath not grown up to a perfect knowledge.**28**

30 But behold, as the seed swelleth, and sprouteth, and beginneth to grow, then you must needs say that the seed is good; for behold it swelleth, and sprouteth, and beginneth to grow.

31 And now, behold, are ye sure that this is a good seed? I say unto you, Yea; for every seed bringeth forth unto its own likeness.

32 Therefore, if a seed groweth it is good, but if it groweth not, behold it is not good, therefore it is cast away.

33 And now, behold, because ye have tried the experiment, and planted the seed, and it swelleth and sprouteth, and beginneth to grow, ye must needs know that the seed is good.

29 Alma 32:34. Gradually, Alma teaches, faith will give way to knowledge as the experimenter observes and verifies the results. Obviously, as with any spiritual growth, some people's faith may be transformed into "sure knowledge" quickly, while others may repeat these spiritual experiments many times as their faith is slowly strengthened and encouraged by the results they observe. Alma notes that eventually, they will achieve "perfect" knowledge, but even then the knowledge is only complete *in that one thing.* For example, people who pray to know whether the Book of Mormon is an inspired document may receive an answer (either immediately or gradually) that it is, because of how its teachings change their lives or bring them closer to God. Eventually, faith will move toward knowledge in that area. But they must still pray and exercise faith on many other spiritual questions, such as the nature of Christ or the reality of the afterlife, repeating this process until faith becomes knowledge in those areas as well. For most Mormons, this is a lifelong process—and even extends beyond this life, as Latter-day Saints believe that they will still be growing and learning spiritual truths in the life to come.

30 Alma 32:37. It's important to keep nourishing the "tree" (growing knowledge) that results from the "seed" (the particle of faith), as it still needs to deepen and extend its roots throughout a person's life. In other words, faith and knowledge continue to expand and intensify throughout the life of the spiritual seeker.

34 And now, behold, is your knowledge perfect? Yea, your knowledge is perfect in that thing, and your faith is dormant;**29** and this because ye know, for ye know that the word hath swelled your souls, and ye also know that it hath sprouted up, that your understanding doth begin to be enlightened, and your mind doth begin to expand.

35 O then, is not this real? I say unto you, Yea, because it is light; and whatsoever is light, is good, because it is discernible, therefore ye must know that it is good; and now behold, after ye have tasted this light is your knowledge perfect?

36 Behold I say unto you, Nay; neither must ye lay aside your faith, for ye have only exercised your faith to plant the seed that ye might try the experiment to know if the seed was good.

37 And behold, as the tree beginneth to grow, ye will say: Let us nourish it with great care, that it may get root, that it may grow up, and bring forth fruit unto us. And now behold, if ye nourish it with much care it will get root, and grow up, and bring forth fruit.**30**

38 But if ye neglect the tree, and take no thought for its nourishment, behold it will not get any root; and when the heat of the sun cometh and scorcheth it, because it hath no root it withers away, and ye pluck it up and cast it out.

39 Now, this is not because the seed was not good, neither is it because the fruit thereof would not be desirable; but it is because your ground is barren, and ye will not nourish the tree, therefore ye cannot have the fruit thereof.

40 And thus, if ye will not nourish the word, looking forward with an eye of faith to the fruit thereof, ye can never pluck of the fruit of the tree of life.

41 But if ye will nourish the word, yea, nourish the tree as it beginneth to grow, by your faith with great diligence, and with patience,

31 Alma 32:42. The "tree" will eventually bear fruit—the pure, holy, and sure knowledge of spiritual truth. What's more, the tables will be turned: This fruit will then nourish and sustain the individual who nourished and sustained the original seed that started the process. Alma teaches that spiritual truth, once tested and verified, is the precious life blood to those patient and diligent people who dare to test the foundations of their faith.

32 Alma 36:1. Alma's instructions to his son Helaman take up chapters 36 and 37, as he is handing over the records. Here, we present chapter 36 in its entirety to demonstrate one of the Book of Mormon's most complex literary devices. It is called *chiasmus*, or *chiasm*, a term that comes from the Greek letter *chi*, which looks like an X. In effect, the structure of chapter 36 is best described by the shape of an X: The beginning and end of a chiasm are parallel, and the parallels continue consistently throughout. In this first verse, for example, the advice to "keep my commandments and ye shall prosper in the land" is repeated verbatim in the final verse of the chapter. In chiasms, such patterns are repeated reliably, with each element having its matching counterpoint: the second idea would have a parallel in the penultimate idea of the chapter; the third idea would have its corresponding verse in the third-to-last section of the chapter, etc. (Note that sometimes, the verse numbers do not correspond precisely; the verse numbers in the Book of Mormon were added later and were not part of the original text.) The pattern continues until we come to the heart of the chiasm—the center of the letter X, so to speak—when we get to the central point of the whole message. In a chiasm, the most important message is located halfway into the text and is the foundation of the rest of the passage.

It is a good idea to read through the entire text of this chapter before delving into the commentary line by line, so that the overall meaning in all the literary parallelism is not lost.

John Welch, a Brigham Young University professor, has done extensive work on Alma 36, and this commentary is adapted from his careful exegesis of the passage and identification of major parallels, to which I have added several more that I have discovered.

looking forward to the fruit thereof, it shall take root; and behold it shall be a tree springing up unto everlasting life.

42 And because of your diligence and your faith and your patience with the word in nourishing it, that it may take root in you, behold, by and by ye shall pluck the fruit thereof, which is most precious, which is sweet above all that is sweet, and which is white above all that is white, yea, and pure above all that is pure; and ye shall feast upon this fruit even until ye are filled, that ye hunger not, neither shall ye thirst.[31]

43 Then, my brethren, ye shall reap the rewards of your faith, and your diligence, and patience, and long-suffering, waiting for the tree to bring forth fruit unto you.

Alma 36

1 My son, give ear to my words; for I swear unto you, that inasmuch as ye shall keep the commandments of God ye shall prosper in the land.[32]

(continued on page 163)

33 Alma 36:2. The phrase "Do as I have done" is picked up in verse 30 but transformed slightly: "Know as I do know." This slight alteration is critical for understanding the meaning of not only Alma 36 but also Alma 32, where we have just seen Alma discuss the importance of putting faith into practice in order to cultivate sure knowledge. The basic notion, then, is that it is through doing that we come to know. Also, note that verse 2's reminder about the *captivity* and *bondage* of the fathers is picked up in verses 28–29.

34 Alma 36:3. Just as the ancestors *trusted* in God and were *delivered* (verse 3), so too does Alma put his *trust* in God and expect *deliverance* (verse 27). And just as God supported the ancestors in all their "trials, and their troubles, and their afflictions," so Alma testifies that he has been supported in his own "trials and troubles" and "afflictions" (verse 27).

35 Alma 36:4. Alma does not "know" this from the teachings of the world, but from the spiritual mind. He says it is "of God." This idea is paralleled in verse 26, where Alma affirms that the knowledge he has is "of God."

36 Alma 36:5. Alma knows these things because he has been "born of God," a phrase he picks up in the corresponding chiastic verse 26, when he remarks that he's not the only one who has attained this knowledge but is one of many who have been born of God because they have personally experienced (tasted and seen) God's goodness.

2 I would that ye should do as I have done,**33** in remembering the captivity of our fathers; for they were in bondage, and none could deliver them except it was the God of Abraham, and the God of Isaac, and the God of Jacob; and he surely did deliver them in their afflictions.

3 And now, O my son Helaman, behold, thou art in thy youth, and therefore, I beseech of thee that thou wilt hear my words and learn of me; for I do know that whosoever shall put their trust in God shall be supported in their trials, and their troubles, and their afflictions, and shall be lifted up at the last day.**34**

4 And I would not that ye think that I know of myself—not of the temporal but of the spiritual, not of the carnal mind but of God.**35**

5 Now, behold, I say unto you, if I had not been born of God**36** I should not have known these things; but God has, by the mouth of his holy angel, made these things known unto me, not of any worthiness of myself.

(continued on page 165)

37 | Alma 36:6–9. In these verses, Alma recounts some of his own history as a former persecutor of the church who then became one of its most ardent and devoted converts. The phrase "seeking to destroy the church" (verse 6) is mirrored by Alma's reflection in verse 24 that since his conversion he has "labored without ceasing, that [he] might bring souls to repentance." Whereas once he tried to tear down the church, his life since he encountered Christ (who is the crux of this chiasm; see verses 17–18) has been about building up the church and bringing God's children into the fold.

38 | Alma 36:10. There is a fascinating parallelism as Alma discusses how the angelic visitation changed his life. For three days after the angel's cease-and-desist order, Alma was struck dumb and says he did not have "the use of [his] limbs." After he comes to understand the atonement of Christ, however, his "limbs did receive their strength again," and he recovered the power of speech, sharing the good news with all who would listen (verse 23).

39 | Alma 36:11–13. As Alma confronts his past, he feels terrible fear and culpability about his many sins. Here, he is so racked with guilt that he can't even hear the further words of the angel; Alma "fell to the earth and … did hear no more" (verse 11). But after coming to understand the glorious truth of Christ's gospel, he is granted a vision of God on his throne (verse 22). Where Alma was once made low by sin, now he is exalted by heavenly grace. Where once he could not even bear to hear the teachings of one angel, now he can hear innumerable angels "singing and praising their God" (verse 22). And where once his "soul was harrowed" by sin and thoughts of hell, now his "soul did long to be there" in heaven with God (verse 22). This last parallel is also made explicit in verses 14–15, when the preconversion Alma cannot bear the thought of one day standing before God for judgment. After discovering Christ's love, he can hardly wait for that day when he will meet God face-to-face.

6 For I went about with the sons of Mosiah, seeking to destroy the church[37] of God; but behold, God sent his holy angel to stop us by the way.

7 And behold, he spake unto us, as it were the voice of thunder, and the whole earth did tremble beneath our feet; and we all fell to the earth, for the fear of the Lord came upon us.

8 But behold, the voice said unto me: Arise. And I arose and stood up, and beheld the angel.

9 And he said unto me: If thou wilt of thyself be destroyed, seek no more to destroy the church of God.

10 And ... I fell to the earth; and it was for the space of three days and three nights that I could not open my mouth, neither had I the use of my limbs.[38]

11 And the angel spake more things unto me, which were heard by my brethren, but I did not hear them; for when I heard the words—If thou wilt be destroyed of thyself, seek no more to destroy the church of God—I was struck with such great fear and amazement lest perhaps I should be destroyed, that I fell to the earth and I did hear no more.[39]

12 But I was racked with eternal torment, for my soul was harrowed up to the greatest degree and racked with all my sins.

13 Yea, I did remember all my sins and iniquities, for which I was tormented with the pains of hell; yea, I saw that I had rebelled against my God, and that I had not kept his holy commandments.

14 Yea, and I had murdered many of his children, or rather led them away unto destruction; yea, and in fine so great had been my iniquities, that the very thought of coming into the presence of my God did rack my soul with inexpressible horror.

40 Alma 36:16. Whereas the preconversion Alma wrestles with the "pains" of a damned soul, later his pains turn to "exquisite and sweet … joy" after redemption from his sins.

41 Alma 36:17. The first half of verse 17 is the last statement before the crux of the chiasm. Here, Alma declares that he was "racked with torment" and "harrowed up by the memory of [his] many sins," while after encountering Christ he immediately "could remember [his] pains no more" and "was harrowed up by the memory of [his] sins no more." For Mormons, as for many Christians, the direct effect of being "born again" (and of being baptized by one who holds the priesthood) is that Christ's atonement has washed away all the penitent's sins, leaving only joy and peace.

42 Alma 36:17–18. Devastated by his sin, Alma remembers what he has heard his father teach about Jesus Christ, the Son of God, who would atone for the sins of the world. Alma's desperate prayer for salvation through Christ is the heart of this entire chiasm and is beautifully similar in simplicity to the Jesus Prayer that has sustained Eastern Orthodox Christians for centuries: "Lord Jesus Christ, have mercy on me, a sinner." The heart of the gospel, for Mormons and other Christians, is humble repentance and total trust in the Lord Jesus Christ.

One interesting aspect of verse 17 is that Alma recalls the truthful teaching of his own father when trying to impart spiritual wisdom to his son. Presumably, Alma wished that he had listened to his father much earlier and more attentively than he had before his conversion—and that his son Helaman would also attend to him. (It's no accident that the first words of this chapter are, "My son, give ear to my words.")

15 Oh, thought I, that I could be banished and become extinct both soul and body, that I might not be brought to stand in the presence of my God, to be judged of my deeds.

16 And now, for three days and for three nights was I racked, even with the pains of a damned soul.**40**

17 And … as I was thus racked with torment, while I was harrowed up by the memory of my many sins,**41** behold, I remembered also to have heard my father prophesy unto the people concerning the coming of one Jesus Christ, a Son of God, to atone for the sins of the world.**42**

18 Now, as my mind caught hold upon this thought, I cried within my heart: O Jesus, thou Son of God, have mercy on me, who am in the gall of bitterness, and am encircled about by the everlasting chains of death.

19 And now, behold, when I thought this, I could remember my pains no more; yea, I was harrowed up by the memory of my sins no more.

20 And oh, what joy, and what marvelous light I did behold; yea, my soul was filled with joy as exceeding as was my pain!

21 Yea, I say unto you, my son, that there could be nothing so exquisite and so bitter as were my pains. Yea, and again I say unto you, my son, that on the other hand, there can be nothing so exquisite and sweet as was my joy.

22 Yea, methought I saw, even as our father Lehi saw, God sitting upon his throne, surrounded with numberless concourses of angels, in the attitude of singing and praising their God; yea, and my soul did long to be there.

23 But behold, my limbs did receive their strength again, and I stood upon my feet, and did manifest unto the people that I had been born of God.

43 Alma 36:27. Alma is referring here to more of his own personal history. As recounted in Alma 9-14, Alma and another man, Amulek, were bound and imprisoned in the city of Ammonihah. The men were saved from incarceration and certain execution when a miraculous earthquake destroyed the walls of the prison, which conveniently fell atop the men's persecutors, killing them. Alma and Amulek were unhurt.

44 Alma 36:29. Again, we see the importance of the phrase "retain in remembrance." Alma wants his son—and us, the modern readers of the Book of Mormon—to always remember the "captivity" of the ancestors.

24 Yea, and from that time even until now, I have labored without ceasing, that I might bring souls unto repentance; that I might bring them to taste of the exceeding joy of which I did taste; that they might also be born of God, and be filled with the Holy Ghost.

25 Yea, and now behold, O my son, the Lord doth give me exceeding great joy in the fruit of my labors;

26 For because of the word which he has imparted unto me, behold, many have been born of God, and have tasted as I have tasted, and have seen eye to eye as I have seen; therefore they do know of these things of which I have spoken, as I do know; and the knowledge which I have is of God.

27 And I have been supported under trials and troubles of every kind, yea, and in all manner of afflictions; yea, God has delivered me from prison, and from bonds, and from death; yea, and I do put my trust in him, and he will still deliver me.**43**

28 And I know that he will raise me up at the last day, to dwell with him in glory; yea, and I will praise him forever, for he has brought our fathers out of Egypt, and he has swallowed up the Egyptians in the Red Sea; and he led them by his power into the promised land; yea, and he has delivered them out of bondage and captivity from time to time.

29 Yea, and he has also brought our fathers out of the land of Jerusalem; and he has also, by his everlasting power, delivered them out of bondage and captivity, from time to time even down to the present day; and I have always retained in remembrance their captivity; yea, and ye also ought to retain in remembrance, as I have done, their captivity.**44**

30 But behold, my son, this is not all; for ye ought to know as I do know, that inasmuch as ye shall keep the commandments of God ye shall

45 Alma 37:32–37. The poetic form that is used on the facing page comes from Grant Hardy, *The Book of Mormon: A Reader's Edition*. Hardy was the first scholar to render this passage in poetic verse, as it probably was intended to be. Readers who are familiar with the biblical book of Proverbs will recognize many of the same elements from proverbial wisdom literature, which often is cast as fatherly advice to a son (or, as is the case with Proverbs 31, a mother's instructions to her son). Here, Alma is still speaking to his son Helaman, exhorting him to model the humility of Christ for the people he will one day lead.

46 Alma 37:35. In biblical wisdom literature, wisdom is sometimes a personified female force; see, for example, Proverbs 8:22–36, where Dame Wisdom speaks of having a hand in the creation. More often, however, it is presented as a general virtue to be cultivated (e.g., Proverbs 14:33 or 3:13–18). This passage in Alma probably has its greatest parallel in Proverbs 4, where a parent advises a child to cling to the right path and hold fast to the way of wisdom. Alma instructs Helaman to learn wisdom by (1) keeping God's commandments, (2) leaning on God for support, and (3) counseling with God in all things. In other words, wisdom is not presented as an instantaneous gift, granted immediately to the one who seeks it out, but as a carefully nurtured quality that is achieved through a lifetime of humble walking with God.

prosper in the land; and ye ought to know also, that inasmuch as ye will not keep the commandments of God ye shall be cut off from his presence. Now this is according to his word.

Alma 37

. . . . .

32   And now, my son, remember the words which I have spoken unto you; trust not those secret plans unto this people, but teach them an everlasting hatred against sin and iniquity.[45]

33 Preach unto them repentance,
    and faith on the Lord Jesus Christ;
teach them to humble themselves
    and to be meek and lowly in heart;
teach them to withstand every temptation of the devil,
    with their faith on the Lord Jesus Christ.

34 Teach them to never be weary of good works,
    but to be meek and lowly in heart;
    for such shall find rest to their souls.

35 O, remember, my son, and learn wisdom[46] in thy youth;
    yea, learn in thy youth to keep the commandments of God.
36 Yea, and cry unto God for all thy support;
    yea, let all thy doings be unto the Lord,
    and whithersoever thou goest let it be in the Lord;
    yea, let thy thoughts be directed unto the Lord;
        yea, let the affections of thy heart be placed upon the Lord forever.

37 Counsel with the Lord in all thy doings,
    and he will direct thee for good;
    yea, when thou liest down at night lie down unto the Lord,
        that he may watch over you in your sleep;

47 Alma 37:38. The small compasslike device that God gave to Nephi centuries earlier, when Nephi was helping to lead his family through the wilderness and across the ocean to the New World (see 1 Nephi 16:9–10).

48 Alma 37:40. The Liahona only worked "by faith," meaning that only a righteous person could exercise it. (During the perilous journey to the Americas, Laman and Lemuel had tied Nephi up and tried to steer the ship themselves with disastrous consequences. The Liahona refused to work for them, and the whole party got lost and almost died in a terrible sea squall; see 1 Nephi 18.)

49 Alma 37:43. One imagines that Helaman is wondering by this time why his father is rehearsing all this ancient history about their ancestors and the Liahona. Alma gets to the heart of it in verse 43, when he suggests that the Liahona story is a "shadow" of an important additional compass. He doesn't want his son to ever become "slothful" in attending to the will of God. As Grant Hardy points out, it's no coincidence that this conversation occurs in the context of the transference of the sacred records from father to son. The scriptures are to be another Liahona, or compass, to guide people to truth.

50 Alma 37:44–45. The inner compass Alma wants his son to consult is the "word of Christ," which includes not only Christ's future teachings but also the very present promise of redemption and forgiveness.

and when thou risest in the morning
> let thy heart be full of thanks unto God;
and if ye do these things,
> ye shall be lifted up at the last day.

38 And now, my son, I have somewhat to say concerning the thing which our fathers call a ball, or director—or our fathers called it Liahona,**47** which is, being interpreted, a compass; and the Lord prepared it.

39 And behold, there cannot any man work after the manner of so curious a workmanship. And behold, it was prepared to show unto our fathers the course which they should travel in the wilderness.

40 And it did work for them according to their faith in God; therefore, if they had faith to believe that God could cause that those spindles should point the way they should go, behold, it was done; therefore they had this miracle, and also many other miracles wrought by the power of God, day by day.**48**

41 Nevertheless, because those miracles were worked by small means it did show unto them marvelous works. They were slothful, and forgot to exercise their faith and diligence and then those marvelous works ceased, and they did not progress in their journey;

42 Therefore, they tarried in the wilderness, or did not travel a direct course, and were afflicted with hunger and thirst, because of their transgressions.

43 And now, my son, I would that ye should understand that these things are not without a shadow; for as our fathers were slothful to give heed to this compass (now these things were temporal) they did not prosper; even so it is with things which are spiritual.**49**

44 For behold, it is as easy to give heed to the word of Christ,**50** which will point to you a straight course to eternal bliss, as it was for our

51 Alma 37:46. Alma is worried that "the easiness of the way" may actually prevent his son and others from paying the serious attention that the spiritual journey deserves. As Christ says in the New Testament, his yoke is easy and his burden is light (Matthew 11:30).

52 Alma 40:1. Here, Alma is speaking not to Helaman but to another son, Corianton. From chapters 38 and 39, it's clear that Alma had just cause to worry about this son, who seems to have lusted after "wicked harlots" and forsaken his call to the ministry. No wonder Corianton seems concerned about the resurrection; his father has already warned him that "behold, ye cannot hide your crimes from God; and except ye repent they will stand as a testimony against you at the last day" (Alma 39:8).

53 Alma 40:11. Alma teaches that there will be an intermediate state between the death of the body and the eventual resurrection of the body. During this time, human spirits are separated from their physical bodies and enter the spirit world.

fathers to give heed to this compass, which would point unto them a straight course to the promised land.

45 And now I say, is there not a type in this thing? For just as surely as this director did bring our fathers, by following its course, to the promised land, shall the words of Christ, if we follow their course, carry us beyond this vale of sorrow into a far better land of promise.

46 O my son, do not let us be slothful because of the easiness of the way;[51] for so was it with our fathers; for so was it prepared for them, that if they would look they might live; even so it is with us. The way is prepared, and if we will look we may live forever.

47 And now, my son, see that ye take care of these sacred things, yea, see that ye look to God and live. Go unto this people and declare the word, and be sober. My son, farewell.

The Spirit World and the Resurrection

Alma 40

1 Now my son, here is somewhat more I would say unto thee; for I perceive that thy mind is worried concerning the resurrection of the dead.[52]

2 Behold, I say unto you, that there is no resurrection—or, I would say, in other words, that this mortal does not put on immortality, this corruption does not put on incorruption—until after the coming of Christ.

. . . . .

11 Now, concerning the state of the soul between death and the resurrection[53]—Behold, it has been made known unto me by an angel, that the spirits of all men, as soon as they are departed from

54 Alma 40:12. One part of the spirit world is a paradise, where those who have been righteous in life will rest from all cares and enjoy peace with God.

55 Alma 40:13. The other part of the spirit world is a prison, where wicked people have an opportunity to repent of their sins. It's confusing that Alma's language (or at least the English translation) refers to this as "outer darkness," because Mormons believe that the temporary state that is spirit prison is actually quite different from the permanent hell that is outer darkness. Spirit prison comes to an end in one of two ways: (1) the prisoner repents sufficiently, accepts the gospel, and can then cross over into spirit paradise to await the resurrection with the righteous, or (2) the prisoner chooses not to repent or accept the gospel and meets the day of resurrection while still in spirit prison. If this is the case, the Lord will judge whether the individual deserves telestial glory (the lowest level of eternal paradise) or banishment into outer darkness, which is essentially an everlasting hell. Most will presumably go to the telestial kingdom. For more on LDS beliefs about the afterlife, see the commentary on 2 Nephi 9:10–12.

One unusual aspect of Mormon belief and practice is the ritual of performing baptisms for the dead. Since Mormons believe that human beings can still make choices in the spirit world and that baptism is a necessary precursor to attaining the fullness of eternal life in the celestial kingdom (the highest heaven), it follows that Mormons also believe that baptism for the dead provides many spirits with a necessary ordinance. Mormons point to the Apostle Paul's comment about baptism for the dead in 1 Corinthians 15:29 as evidence that it was a spiritual practice of the first-century Christian church and has a biblical precedent.

It's important to note that just because a Mormon can be baptized by proxy on some particular spirit's behalf, that spirit has the choice of accepting or rejecting the ordinance. Merely having the ordinance performed does not "make" a person a Mormon against his or her will. It merely opens the door for that person to have every spiritual opportunity available when making crucial choices (continued on page 178)

this mortal body, yea, the spirits of all men, whether they be good or evil, are taken home to that God who gave them life.

12 And then shall it come to pass, that the spirits of those who are righteous are received into a state of happiness, which is called paradise,**54** a state of rest, a state of peace, where they shall rest from all their troubles and from all care, and sorrow.

13 And then shall it come to pass, that the spirits of the wicked, yea, who are evil—for behold, they have no part nor portion of the Spirit of the Lord; for behold, they chose evil works rather than good; therefore the spirit of the devil did enter into them, and take possession of their house—and these shall be cast out into outer darkness;**55** there shall be weeping, and wailing, and gnashing of teeth, and this because of their own iniquity, being led captive by the will of the devil.

14 Now this is the state of the souls of the wicked, yea, in darkness, and a state of awful, fearful looking for the fiery indignation of the wrath of God upon them; thus they remain in this state, as well as the righteous in paradise, until the time of their resurrection.

. . . . .

(*continued on page 179*)

about his or her eternal fate. Mormons believe that individuals still continue to exercise their agency, even in the afterlife.

56 Alma 40:23. At the day of resurrection, people's bodies and spirits will be once again reunited. However, this time the body will be "perfect," which to Mormons means being free of disease, corruption, or physical death.

57 Alma 40:26. This "awful death" Alma speaks about is outer darkness. Although all people will be given every opportunity to repent of their sins and accept the love of God and His Son, Jesus Christ, a small portion of the human race will choose this cursed fate for themselves. It is very interesting that this concept of hell mentions no fires or pitchforks or devils; what Alma suggests is instead a hell in the worst possible interior sense. Those people who prefer banishment in outer darkness to repenting of their sins will be "consigned to partake of the fruits of their labors or their works, which have been evil." One imagines that these individuals might be forced to relive their own actions over and over again and possibly also to feel how the "fruits" of their evil deeds could have affected others. This is of course speculation, but such a karmic future would certainly fit Alma's definition of a "bitter cup."

58 Alma 41:1. "Restoration" here equals resurrection, i.e., the restoration of the body with the soul.

23 The soul shall be restored to the body, and the body to the soul; yea, and every limb and joint shall be restored to its body; yea, even a hair of the head shall not be lost; but all things shall be restored to their proper and perfect frame.[56]

24 And now, my son, this is the restoration of which has been spoken by the mouths of the prophets—

25 And then shall the righteous shine forth in the kingdom of God.

26 But behold, an awful death[57] cometh upon the wicked; for they die as to things pertaining to things of righteousness; for they are unclean, and no unclean thing can inherit the kingdom of God; but they are cast out, and consigned to partake of the fruits of their labors or their works, which have been evil; and they drink the dregs of a bitter cup.

Alma 41

1 And now, my son, I have somewhat to say concerning the restoration[58] of which has been spoken; for behold, some have wrested the scriptures, and have gone far astray because of this thing. And I perceive that thy mind has been worried also concerning this thing. But behold, I will explain it unto thee.

2 I say unto thee, my son, that the plan of restoration is requisite with the justice of God; for it is requisite that all things should be restored to their proper order. Behold, it is requisite and just, according to the power and resurrection of Christ, that the soul of man should be restored to its body, and that every part of the body should be restored to itself.

3 And it is requisite with the justice of God that men should be judged according to their works; and if their works were good in this life,

59 Alma 41:4. Here, there is a pun on the word *restoration*; just as the body is restored to its perfect frame at the resurrection, evil and unrepentant people's works will be "restored" to them at the last day. See also verse 13.

60 Alma 41:10. Alma clarifies that people will not be resurrected in their sins. If they have not repented and received Christ's forgiveness, they won't receive the "restoration" of the full resurrection and spiritual exaltation.

61 Alma 41:13. To restore something is not to create it anew, but to return it to its original pristine condition. Alma further explains that people's good or evil works will be "restored" to them at the last day.

and the desires of their hearts were good, that they should also, at the last day, be restored unto that which is good.

4 And if their works are evil they shall be restored unto them for evil.**59** Therefore, all things shall be restored to their proper order, every thing to its natural frame—mortality raised to immortality, corruption to incorruption—raised to endless happiness to inherit the kingdom of God, or to endless misery to inherit the kingdom of the devil, the one on one hand, the other on the other—

. . . . .

10 Do not suppose, because it has been spoken concerning restoration, that ye shall be restored from sin to happiness.**60** Behold, I say unto you, wickedness never was happiness.

11 And now, my son, all men that are in a state of nature, or I would say, in a carnal state, are in the gall of bitterness and in the bonds of iniquity; they are without God in the world, and they have gone contrary to the nature of God; therefore, they are in a state contrary to the nature of happiness.

12 And now behold, is the meaning of the word restoration to take a thing of a natural state and place it in an unnatural state, or to place it in a state opposite to its nature?

13 O, my son, this is not the case; but the meaning of the word restoration is to bring back again evil for evil, or carnal for carnal, or devilish for devilish—good for that which is good; righteous for that which is righteous; just for that which is just; merciful for that which is merciful.**61**

14 Therefore, my son, see that you are merciful unto your brethren; deal justly, judge righteously, and do good continually; and if ye do all these things then shall ye receive your reward; yea, ye shall have mercy restored unto you again; ye shall have justice restored unto

62 Alma 41:14. Just as the prophet Micah encouraged people to "do justly ... love mercy ... and walk humbly" with God (Micah 6:8), Alma exhorts his son to deal justly and mercifully with all.

you again; ye shall have a righteous judgment restored unto you again; and ye shall have good rewarded unto you again.**62**

15 For that which ye do send out shall return unto you again, and be restored; therefore, the word restoration more fully condemneth the sinner, and justifieth him not at all.

1 3 Nephi 11:1. We now skip ahead more than a hundred years from Alma's advice to his sons (ca. 73 BCE) to the coming of Christ to the New World (sometime between 30 and 35 CE). Prior to this scene, there have been tumultuous and cataclysmic portents; storms, earthquakes, and fires have destroyed several Nephite cities. This destruction happened in the New World at the same time that Christ was being crucified in the old. Then a thick darkness covered the land in the New World for three days (coincident to the time that Christ was in the tomb). During this time, Christ's voice spoke to the people, urging them to repent and give their hearts to him. In his teachings, he identifies them as the house of Israel, tells them that they have been saved from the devastation because they were more righteous than their neighbors, and promises to come among them. Some time later, he visits with approximately twenty-five hundred Nephite men, women, and children for three days at the temple in Bountiful. (The text is not specific about exactly when this happened, or how much time has passed, but this visit occurred at least after the forty days that Christ spent after his resurrection ministering with his apostles in and around Jerusalem, as recorded in the New Testament. It may have been even later, especially if Christ visited other people around the globe, as the Book of Mormon teaches.)

6 □ The Third Book of Nephi

Jesus Teaches the Nephites

3 Nephi 11

1 And now ... there were a great multitude gathered together, of the people of Nephi, round about the temple which was in the land Bountiful;[1] and they were marveling and wondering one with another, and were showing one to another the great and marvelous change which had taken place.

2 And they were also conversing about this Jesus Christ, of whom the sign had been given concerning his death.

3 And ... while they were thus conversing one with another, they heard a voice as if it came out of heaven; and they cast their eyes round about, for they understood not the voice which they heard; and it was not a harsh voice, neither was it a loud voice; nevertheless, and notwithstanding it being a small voice it did pierce them that did hear to the center, insomuch that there was no part of their frame that it did not cause to quake; yea, it did pierce them to the very soul, and did cause their hearts to burn.

4 And ... again they heard the voice, and they understood it not.

5 And again the third time they did hear the voice, and did open their ears to hear it; and their eyes were towards the sound thereof; and they did look steadfastly towards heaven, from whence the sound came.

2 3 Nephi 11:5–6. The people hear the voice speaking, but they don't understand its words until the third time. This has other parallels in scripture; in the Old Testament/Hebrew Bible, for example, Eli does not understand that it is God's voice calling Samuel until the third time the boy tells Eli that he heard a voice calling his name (1 Samuel 3:1–9). And in Joseph Smith's account of the coming forth of the Book of Mormon (now canonized as part of the LDS book of scripture called the Pearl of Great Price), the angel Moroni tells Joseph the same information about the golden plates' history and significance several times with almost no variation. It would seem that people need time to adjust to hearing divine voices and receiving angelic visitations; they are so overwhelmed at first that they are liable to miss the all-important spiritual message that is to be imparted. God and his messengers repeat their teachings so that people will have a chance to attend carefully to the words.

3 3 Nephi 11:7. This is very similar to God's introduction of his Son Jesus Christ in the New Testament (see Mark 1:11 or Matthew 3:17), as he is being baptized at the very start of his ministry. However, the Book of Mormon adds the supplementary phrase "in whom I have glorified my name." Since Christ's visit to the Nephites occurs after his ministry, death, and resurrection, this means that all these events have succeeded in glorifying the name of the Father.

4 3 Nephi 11:10. In the New Testament, particularly in Mark, Jesus is rather reticent about his identity as the Messiah and the Son of God. Here, by contrast, the first words out of his mouth are to introduce himself as the Messiah, or the Christ. He proclaims that he is the fulfillment of prophecy, which would have been significant news to the Nephites, who had heard many prophecies of this Christ who would one day come.

6 And behold, the third time they did understand the voice which they heard;[2] and it said unto them:

7 Behold my Beloved Son, in whom I am well pleased, in whom I have glorified my name[3]—hear ye him.

8 And ... as they understood they cast their eyes up again towards heaven; and behold, they saw a Man descending out of heaven; and he was clothed in a white robe; and he came down and stood in the midst of them; and the eyes of the whole multitude were turned upon him, and they durst not open their mouths, even one to another, and wist not what it meant, for they thought it was an angel that had appeared unto them.

9 And ... he stretched forth his hand and spake unto the people, saying:

10 Behold, I am Jesus Christ, whom the prophets testified shall come into the world.[4]

11 And behold, I am the light and the life of the world; and I have drunk out of that bitter cup which the Father hath given me, and have glorified the Father in taking upon me the sins of the world, in the which I have suffered the will of the Father in all things from the beginning.

12 And ... when Jesus had spoken these words the whole multitude fell to the earth; for they remembered that it had been prophesied among them that Christ should show himself unto them after his ascension into heaven.

13 And ... the Lord spake unto them saying:

(continued on page 189)

5   3 Nephi 11:14. In Mormonism, there is a "law of witnesses" that suggests God will manifest spiritual truth in at least two ways. For instance, when Jesus is baptized in the New Testament, God the Father speaks and the Holy Ghost appears as a dove—two separate witnesses of Christ's calling and mission. Mormons believe that the Book of Mormon itself is "another testament," or witness, of Jesus Christ, which stands alongside the Bible offering additional testimony and information about the Savior. Here, the law of witnesses can be seen in the fact that Christ uses *both* sight and touch to convince the Nephites that he has died. They see the wounds, and he invites them to touch his side, hands, and feet.

6   3 Nephi 11:15. LDS Apostle Jeffrey R. Holland notes that in the Book of Mormon, "It is a significant and hopeful fact that it is the wounded Christ who comes to our rescue." Since Christ is the only person in history to be brought back to life without later succumbing to a second physical death (Lazarus in the New Testament, for instance, was raised from the dead but presumably died of other causes later), and we know from other Book of Mormon teachings that to be resurrected means to inherit a perfect physical body, it must follow that the resurrected Christ *chose* to appear before the Nephites in his wounded state. Elder Holland writes, "Even though the power of the Resurrection could have—and undoubtedly one day will have—completely restored and made new the wounds from the crucifixion, nevertheless Christ chose to retain those wounds for a purpose, including for his appearance in the last days when he will show those marks and reveal that he was wounded 'in the house of [his] friends.'"

7   3 Nephi 11:22. Jesus officially institutes the ordinance of baptism among the Nephites and gives Nephi and others the authority to baptize the people. In Mormonism, baptism is considered an essential ordinance and must be performed by one who holds the sacred priesthood. Interestingly, one of the few bits of advice Christ gives on the issue of baptism is the clear warning that there should be "no disputations" about the issue, an admonition he repeats *(continued on page 190)*

14 Arise and come forth unto me, that ye may thrust your hands into my side, and also that ye may feel the prints of the nails in my hands and in my feet,**5** that ye may know that I am the God of Israel, and the God of the whole earth, and have been slain for the sins of the world.

15 And ... the multitude went forth, and thrust their hands into his side, and did feel the prints of the nails in his hands and in his feet; and this they did do, going forth one by one until they had all gone forth, and did see with their eyes and did feel with their hands, and did know of a surety and did bear record, that it was he, of whom it was written by the prophets, that should come.**6**

16 And when they had all gone forth and had witnessed for themselves, they did cry out with one accord, saying:

17 Hosanna! Blessed be the name of the Most High God! And they did fall down at the feet of Jesus, and did worship him.

18 And ... he spake unto Nephi (for Nephi was among the multitude) and he commanded him that he should come forth.

19 And Nephi arose and went forth, and bowed himself before the Lord and did kiss his feet.

20 And the Lord commanded him that he should arise. And he arose and stood before him.

Baptism

21 And the Lord said unto him: I give unto you power that ye shall baptize this people when I am again ascended into heaven.

22 And again the Lord called others, and said unto them likewise; and he gave unto them power to baptize. And he said unto them: On this wise shall ye baptize; and there shall be no disputations among you.**7**

in verse 28. Mormons believe that the Book of Mormon is intended for our times and contains those specific teachings that would be most relevant for today, so Mormon, the editor, may have chosen to include this bit of Christ's teaching (out of many others that went unrecorded) because contentions over baptism have characterized some modern Christian groups.

8 3 Nephi 11:25. Similar words are said at every LDS baptism, just before the person getting baptized goes into the water. Note that although Mormons believe in the three beings of the godhead—the Father, Son, and Holy Ghost—they do not subscribe to other Christians' belief that all three beings are actually three-in-one, comprising a holy Trinity. Latter-day Saints do not believe that the idea of the Trinity has a solid grounding in scripture. Instead, they see the beings of the godhead as three separate personages who are wholly united in purpose and ministry (see verse 27).

9 3 Nephi 11:26. Mormons baptize by full immersion. Baptism can occur in any body of water, such as a river, a lake, or even a swimming pool, but it typically happens in a baptismal font in the local ward (congregation) meetinghouse.

10 3 Nephi 11:27. Sometimes, the language of the Book of Mormon seems to suggest a Trinitarian worldview, but as we saw in the previous note, Mormons do not believe that the Father, Son, and Holy Ghost are *literally* one being. Here, Jesus points to their intimate connection and shared purpose ("I am in the Father, and the Father in me") but does not insist that they are a single essence.

23 Verily I say unto you, that whoso repenteth of his sins through your words and desireth to be baptized in my name, on this wise shall ye baptize them—Behold, ye shall go down and stand in the water, and in my name shall ye baptize them.

24 And now behold, these are the words which ye shall say, calling them by name, saying:

25 Having authority given me of Jesus Christ, I baptize you in the name of the Father, and of the Son, and of the Holy Ghost. Amen.[8]

26 And then shall ye immerse[9] them in the water, and come forth again out of the water.

27 And after this manner shall ye baptize in my name; for behold, verily I say unto you, that the Father, and the Son, and the Holy Ghost are one; and I am in the Father, and the Father in me, and the Father and I are one.[10]

28 And according as I have commanded you thus shall ye baptize. And there shall be no disputations among you, as there have hitherto been; neither shall there be disputations among you concerning the points of my doctrine, as there have hitherto been.

. . . . .

The House of Israel

3 Nephi 15

. . . . .

11 And now ... when Jesus had spoken these words, he said unto those twelve whom he had chosen:

11 3 Nephi 15:11–12. Just as he did in and around Jerusalem, Jesus selects twelve disciples to be the spiritual leaders of the Nephites. He also identifies the Nephites as "a remnant of the house of Joseph," meaning that Lehi was descended from the Joseph of the book of Genesis, one of Jacob's twelve sons. Interestingly, in the Old Testament, Jacob adopts Joseph's two sons Ephraim and Manasseh as his own, drawing them into the original twelve tribes of Israel (Genesis 48:5).

Today, most Mormons can obtain a once-in-a-lifetime formal blessing called a "patriarchal blessing," performed by a regional leader who is specifically called and set apart to the task. One of the most unusual features of a patriarchal blessing is a declaration of lineage, proclaiming the modern-day Latter-day Saint to be a member of one of the original tribes of Israel. Many Mormons are declared to be of the tribe of Ephraim, perhaps because that tribe is given particularly important blessings and responsibilities (see Genesis 48:19–20).

12 3 Nephi 15:13. The Savior clarifies that "this is the land" of this tribe's inheritance. In the Old Testament/Hebrew Bible, frequent mention is made of the exact land each tribe would inherit as its portion. (The exception to this rule is the tribe of Levi, whose members were appointed as priests over the people and did not have a designated homeland for themselves.) Here, the Savior continues introducing the Nephites to the concept of their "tribe" by following ancient precedent in apportioning them a particular land.

13 3 Nephi 15:19. Jesus is referring here to the fact that Lehi's family fled Jerusalem because of the city's sin, which resulted in the destruction of the temple and the exile of many people to Babylon. Jesus teaches the Nephites that their ancestor Lehi was separated from the rest of the House of Israel because of "their" iniquity—a pronoun that is repeated in this verse and again in the next. In other words, these people are descended from a righteous remnant and have a noble heritage (whatever they have done in the subsequent generations).

12 Ye are my disciples; and ye are a light unto this people, who are a remnant of the house of Joseph.**11**

13 And behold, this is the land of your inheritance;**12** and the Father hath given it unto you.

14 And not at any time hath the Father given me commandment that I should tell it unto your brethren at Jerusalem.

15 Neither at any time hath the Father given me commandment that I should tell unto them concerning the other tribes of the house of Israel, whom the Father hath led away out of the land.

16 This much did the Father command me, that I should tell unto them:

17 That other sheep I have which are not of this fold; them also I must bring, and they shall hear my voice; and there shall be one fold, and one shepherd.

18 And now, because of stiffneckedness and unbelief they understood not my word; therefore I was commanded to say no more of the Father concerning this thing unto them.

19 But, verily, I say unto you that the Father hath commanded me, and I tell it unto you, that ye were separated from among them because of their iniquity;**13** therefore it is because of their iniquity that they know not of you.

20 And verily, I say unto you again that the other tribes hath the Father separated from them; and it is because of their iniquity that they know not of them.

21 And verily I say unto you, that ye are they of whom I said: Other sheep I have which are not of this fold; them also I must bring, and they shall hear my voice; and there shall be one fold, and one shepherd.

14 3 Nephi 15:24. For more on the law of witnesses, see the commentary on 3 Nephi 11:14.

15 3 Nephi 17:3. The Savior is ready to conclude his first day of teaching by encouraging the Nephites to go home and pray about all they have learned and heard.

16 3 Nephi 17:4. Mormons believe that the Nephites were probably not the only people Christ visited in the time following his resurrection. Here, he refers to other "lost tribes" that the world has forgotten but that the Father remembers.

22 And they understood me not, for they supposed it had been the Gentiles; for they understood not that the Gentiles should be converted through their preaching.

23 And they understood me not that I said they shall hear my voice; and they understood me not that the Gentiles should not at any time hear my voice—that I should not manifest myself unto them save it were by the Holy Ghost.

24 But behold, ye have both heard my voice, and seen me;**14** and ye are my sheep, and ye are numbered among those whom the Father hath given me.

Jesus's Compassion

3 Nephi 17

1 Behold, now ... when Jesus had spoken these words he looked round about again on the multitude, and he said unto them: Behold, my time is at hand.

2 I perceive that ye are weak, that ye cannot understand all my words which I am commanded of the Father to speak unto you at this time.

3 Therefore, go ye unto your homes, and ponder upon the things which I have said, and ask of the Father, in my name, that ye may understand, and prepare your minds for the morrow, and I come unto you again.**15**

4 But now I go unto the Father, and also to show myself unto the lost tribes of Israel, for they are not lost unto the Father, for he knoweth whither he hath taken them.**16**

5 And ... when Jesus had thus spoken, he cast his eyes round about again on the multitude, and beheld they were in tears, and did look

17 3 Nephi 17:5–7. Although Jesus was ready to finish his teaching for the day, he is filled with compassion for the people and agrees to "tarry a little longer" and heal their sick. Harvard Divinity School professor Krister Stendahl has observed some distinct differences between 3 Nephi and the Gospel of Matthew. In Matthew, Jesus healed those who were brought to him on a case-by-case basis, but in 3 Nephi he invites "all them that were afflicted in any manner." Critics have argued that this reflects the desire of Joseph Smith—whom they believe to be the "real" author of the Book of Mormon—to depict Jesus in an even more grand and supernatural way than he is presented in the New Testament. Mormon apologists counter that this reflects the Savior's postresurrection divinity as opposed to the unique blend of humanity and divinity that characterized his mortal life.

steadfastly upon him as if they would ask him to tarry a little longer with them.

6 And he said unto them: Behold, my bowels are filled with compassion towards you.

7 Have ye any that are sick among you?**17** Bring them hither. Have ye any that are lame, or blind, or halt, or maimed, or leprous, or that are withered, or that are deaf, or that are afflicted in any manner? Bring them hither and I will heal them, for I have compassion upon you; my bowels are filled with mercy.

8 For I perceive that ye desire that I should show unto you what I have done unto your brethren at Jerusalem, for I see that your faith is sufficient that I should heal you.

9 And ... when he had thus spoken, all the multitude, with one accord, did go forth with their sick and their afflicted, and their lame, and with their blind, and with their dumb, and with all them that were afflicted in any manner; and he did heal them every one as they were brought forth unto him.

10 And they did all, both they who had been healed and they who were whole, bow down at his feet, and did worship him; and as many as could come for the multitude did kiss his feet, insomuch that they did bathe his feet with their tears.

11 And ... he commanded that their little children should be brought.

12 So they brought their little children and set them down upon the ground round about him, and Jesus stood in the midst; and the multitude gave way till they had all been brought unto him.

. . . . .

(continued on page 199)

18 3 Nephi 17:21. The Savior's love and compassion are demonstrated by the fact that the Nephites' faith moves him to tears. Note that afterward he blesses all the children individually.

19 3 Nephi 17:24. This miraculous spiritual manifestation is similar to the supernatural descent of the Holy Spirit described in Acts 2:1–4. Here, though, the miracle is particularly directed to the "little ones"— the children who have just been blessed by Jesus—and the people witness angels descending from heaven.

Jesus Blesses the Children

18 And … when Jesus had made an end of praying unto the Father, he arose; but so great was the joy of the multitude that they were overcome.

19 And … Jesus spake unto them, and bade them arise.

20 And they arose from the earth, and he said unto them: Blessed are ye because of your faith. And now behold, my joy is full.

21 And when he had said these words, he wept, and the multitude bare record of it, and he took their little children, one by one, and blessed them, and prayed unto the Father for them.**18**

22 And when he had done this he wept again;

23 And he spake unto the multitude, and said unto them: Behold your little ones.

24 And as they looked to behold they cast their eyes towards heaven, and they saw the heavens open, and they saw angels descending out of heaven as it were in the midst of fire; and they came down and encircled those little ones about, and they were encircled about with fire; and the angels did minister unto them.**19**

25 And the multitude did see and hear and bear record; and they know that their record is true for they all of them did see and hear, every man for himself; and they were in number about two thousand and five hundred souls; and they did consist of men, women, and children.

(continued on page 201)

20 3 Nephi 18:1. In the New Testament, Jesus institutes the ritual that Christians call the Last Supper, the Eucharist, or Holy Communion on the eve of his arrest and trial. In the Book of Mormon, the event isn't shadowed by an impending betrayal; Jesus simply shares the wine and the bread and instructs them to follow his example, making sure that the ritual (which Mormons call "the sacrament") is performed by one who has authority.

21 3 Nephi 18:7. Mormons view the sacrament as a "remembrance" of the Savior's love and sacrifice, which is more in line with Protestant thinking than it is with Roman Catholic theology. Mormons do not believe that the bread miraculously transforms into Christ's body at the moment of consecration, as Catholics do.

22 3 Nephi 18:8. Although Mormons drank wine with the sacrament into the twentieth century, for approximately the last hundred years they have substituted water for wine in their services. This is in line with today's strict interpretation of the "Word of Wisdom," or the health code that is laid out in Doctrine and Covenants 89. Although members of the nineteenth-century Church sometimes drank modest amounts of wine and beer, contemporary Mormons abstain entirely from alcohol and also eschew illicit drugs, tobacco, coffee, and tea.

The Sacrament

3 Nephi 18

1 And ... Jesus commanded his disciples that they should bring forth some bread and wine unto him.[20]

2 And while they were gone for bread and wine, he commanded the multitude that they should sit themselves down upon the earth.

3 And when the disciples had come with bread and wine, he took of the bread and brake and blessed it; and he gave unto the disciples and commanded that they should eat.

4 And when they had eaten and were filled, he commanded that they should give unto the multitude.

5 And when the multitude had eaten and were filled, he said unto the disciples: Behold there shall one be ordained among you, and to him will I give power that he shall break bread and bless it and give it unto the people of my church, unto all those who shall believe and be baptized in my name.

6 And this shall ye always observe to do, even as I have done, even as I have broken bread and blessed it and given it unto you.

7 And this shall ye do in remembrance[21] of my body, which I have shown unto you. And it shall be a testimony unto the Father that ye do always remember me. And if ye do always remember me ye shall have my Spirit to be with you.

8 And ... when he said these words, he commanded his disciples that they should take of the wine[22] of the cup and drink of it, and that they should also give unto the multitude that they might drink of it.

9 And ... they did so, and did drink of it and were filled; and they gave unto the multitude, and they did drink, and they were filled.

23 3 Nephi 18:11. The Savior ties the idea of remembering him with the gift of the Holy Ghost. Mormons believe that when they take the sacrament—which they do nearly every Sunday—they renew their baptismal covenant to take upon themselves the name of Christ. This is a weighty responsibility, but Mormons believe that partaking of the sacrament gives them the strength to bear the honor of the Savior's name and become more like him.

24 3 Nephi 18:19. When Mormons pray, they always address Heavenly Father and close the prayer along the lines of, "...in the name of Jesus Christ, amen." This traces back to this verse in 3 Nephi, when the Savior instructs the Nephites to pray to the Father in the name of the Son.

25 3 Nephi 18:20. The phrase "which is right" qualifies the notion that people will simply receive whatever they pray for. Mormons feel that so-called prosperity theology, which teaches people to expect whatever they pray for—whether it be a luxurious house or a job promotion—is wrongheaded. If they are not praying for righteous things (typically defined as those things that will bless others and serve God's kingdom), then they are not praying as the Savior instructed. People have no right to expect blessings that will merely further selfish impulses, no matter how great their faith.

26 3 Nephi 18:21. Mormons try to pray in their families regularly (ideally, every day) in addition to the private prayer they engage in as individuals.

10 And when the disciples had done this, Jesus said unto them: Blessed are ye for this thing which ye have done, for this is fulfilling my commandments, and this doth witness unto the Father that ye are willing to do that which I have commanded you.

11 And this shall ye always do to those who repent and are baptized in my name; and ye shall do it in remembrance of my blood, which I have shed for you, that ye may witness unto the Father that ye do always remember me. And if ye do always remember me ye shall have my Spirit to be with you.[23]

. . . . .

On Prayer

19 Therefore ye must always pray unto the Father in my name;[24]

20 And whatsoever ye shall ask the Father in my name, which is right,[25] believing that ye shall receive, behold it shall be given unto you.

21 Pray in your families[26] unto the Father, always in my name, that your wives and your children may be blessed.

(continued on page 205)

27 3 Nephi 18:22–23. The Book of Mormon again teaches that believers have no right to refuse access to anyone who wants to worship with them in their regular meetings. Mormons welcome all people to their Sunday services in ward (congregational) meetinghouses all over the world. However, their special temples are reserved only for worthy Latter-day Saints and are not open to the public except for a short time prior to their dedication. There are now more than one hundred thirty LDS temples in operation or under construction around the world.

28 3 Nephi 18:35–39. Jesus leaves the Nephites after his brief sojourn with them, teaching and healing. Before leaving, he gives his disciples the gift of the Holy Ghost and the power to pass that gift along to others. Finally, he ascends to heaven in a cloud.

22 And behold, ye shall meet together oft; and ye shall not forbid any man from coming unto you when ye shall meet together,**27** but suffer them that they may come unto you and forbid them not;

23 But ye shall pray for them, and shall not cast them out; and if it so be that they come unto you oft ye shall pray for them unto the Father, in my name.

24 Therefore, hold up your light that it may shine unto the world. Behold I am the light which ye shall hold up—that which ye have seen me do. Behold ye see that I have prayed unto the Father, and ye all have witnessed.

. . . . .

Jesus Ascends to Heaven

35 And now I go unto the Father, because it is expedient that I should go unto the Father for your sakes.

36 And ... when Jesus had made an end of these sayings, he touched with his hand the disciples whom he had chosen, one by one, even until he had touched them all, and spake unto them as he touched them.

37 And the multitude heard not the words which he spake, therefore they did not bear record; but the disciples bare record that he gave them power to give the Holy Ghost. And I will show unto you hereafter that this record is true.

38 And ... when Jesus had touched them all, there came a cloud and overshadowed the multitude that they could not see Jesus.

39 And while they were overshadowed he departed from them, and ascended into heaven. And the disciples saw and did bear record that he ascended again into heaven.**28**

1 Mormon 6:5. After the Savior's visit to the Nephites, they enjoyed a brief golden age of peace and prosperity. During this period, there was one church with no division between Nephite and Lamanite; all the people united in a common faith and pooled all of their economic resources, sharing everything. Unfortunately, it did not last. Around the turn of the third century CE (ca. 201), the old class lines and divisions began to reassert themselves. Believers in the true religion were persecuted and killed. Before long, it wasn't just the Lamanites who were wicked, but many among the Nephites as well, who succumbed to the sins of pride and unbelief. Here in chapter 6, the last of the righteous Nephites gather for a final battle against their enemies. The year is about 385 CE.

2 Mormon 6:6. Knowing that the end is near, Mormon (a Nephite military captain and spiritual leader) explains that he has edited the records of his ancestors (his work consists of most of our current Book of Mormon) and has given his son Moroni only that small portion of it that he thinks will be useful. Although most nineteenth-century Mormons believed that the "hill Cumorah" was located in western New York State, where the prophet Joseph Smith was led to discover the record in the 1820s, many now hold that the actual battle site of Cumorah is located much further south, possibly somewhere in Central America. Mormon's son Moroni, we know from the text, spent more than three decades wandering alone trying to flee the Lamanites, so it is very plausible that he took his small abridgment of the records and buried them in what became western New York. Although there is a place in modern-day New York that Mormons call "the Hill Cumorah," this is almost certainly not the same hill that is mentioned as the site of the Nephites' final battle.

7 □ The Book of Mormon

The Close of the Age

Mormon 6

. . . . .

5 And when three hundred and eighty and four years had passed away, we had gathered in all the remainder of our people unto the land of Cumorah.**1**

6 And ... when we had gathered in all our people in one to the land of Cumorah, behold I, Mormon, began to be old; and knowing it to be the last struggle of my people, and having been commanded of the Lord that I should not suffer the records which had been handed down by our fathers, which were sacred, to fall into the hands of the Lamanites, (for the Lamanites would destroy them) therefore I made this record out of the plates of Nephi, and hid up in the hill Cumorah all the records which had been entrusted to me by the hand of the Lord, save it were these few plates which I gave unto my son Moroni.**2**

7 And ... my people, with their wives and their children, did now behold the armies of the Lamanites marching towards them; and with that awful fear of death which fills the breasts of all the wicked, did they await to receive them.

8 And ... they came to battle against us, and every soul was filled with terror because of the greatness of their numbers.

3 | Mormon 6:16–20. Known as "Mormon's lamentation," this heartrending cry shows Mormon's anguish on behalf of his people, who abandoned the love of Christ. The poetic meter shown here is taken from Grant Hardy, *The Book of Mormon: A Reader's Edition.*

9 And ... they did fall upon my people with the sword, and with the bow, and with the arrow, and with the ax, and with all manner of weapons of war.

. . . . .

16　And my soul was rent with anguish, because of the slain of my people, and I cried[3]

17 O ye fair ones,
　　how could ye have departed from the ways of the Lord!
O ye fair ones,
　　how could ye have rejected that Jesus,
　　who stood with open arms to receive you!
18 Behold, if ye had not done this, ye would not have fallen.
　　But behold, ye are fallen, and I mourn your loss.
19 O ye fair sons and daughters,
　　ye fathers and mothers,
　　ye husbands and wives,
ye fair ones,
　　how is it that ye could have fallen!
20 But behold, ye are gone,
　　and my sorrows cannot bring your return.

21 And the day soon cometh that your mortal must put on immortality, and these bodies which are now moldering in corruption must soon become incorruptible bodies; and then ye must stand before the judgment-seat of Christ to be judged according to your works and if it so be that ye are righteous, then are ye blessed with your fathers who have gone before you.

22 O that ye had repented before this great destruction had come upon you. But behold, ye are gone, and the Father, yea, the Eternal Father of heaven, knoweth your state; and he doeth with you according to his justice and mercy.

[4] Mormon 8:1–4. Moroni, Mormon's son, inherits the task of finishing the record after Mormon is killed in battle. It's now around 400 or 401 CE, the close of the era chronicled in the Book of Mormon.

[5] Mormon 8:12. Moroni acknowledges that the record contains "imperfections," but we don't know what those are. Judging from the following sentence, he seems to feel that the record is imperfect because there is so much of the story that he's had to omit. Still, he knows that it will be of great value to readers even with the "imperfections."

[6] Mormon 8:16. "He that shall bring this thing to light" refers to Joseph Smith.

Mormon 8

1 Behold I, Moroni, do finish the record of my father, Mormon.**4** Behold, I have but few things to write, which things I have been commanded by my father.

2 And now ... after the great and tremendous battle at Cumorah, behold, the Nephites who had escaped into the country southward were hunted by the Lamanites, until they were all destroyed.

3 And my father also was killed by them, and I even remain alone to write the sad tale of the destruction of my people. But behold, they are gone, and I fulfil the commandment of my father. And whether they will slay me, I know not.

4 Therefore I will write and hide up the records in the earth; and whither I go it mattereth not.

. . . . .

12 And whoso receiveth this record, and shall not condemn it because of the imperfections which are in it, the same shall know of greater things than these.**5** Behold, I am Moroni; and were it possible, I would make all things known unto you.

. . . . .

16 And blessed be he that shall bring this thing to light;**6** for it shall be brought out of darkness unto light, according to the word of God; yea, it shall be brought out of the earth, and it shall shine forth out of darkness, and come unto the knowledge of the people; and it shall be done by the power of God.

17 And if there be faults they be the faults of a man. But behold, we know no fault; nevertheless God knoweth all things; therefore, he that condemneth, let him be aware lest he shall be in danger of hell fire.

. . . . .

7 | Mormon 8:34. In one of the Book of Mormon's most stunning revelations, Moroni declares that he has been privileged to witness in a vision the future circumstances of the coming forth of the record he's completing. His perspective of time seems to be spiritual, since the roughly fifteen hundred years that elapsed between his final writings (ca. 421 CE) and his first visit in angelic form to Joseph Smith (1826 CE) would not be considered brief by most people. Yet he says the day "must shortly come" when the records will come forth.

8 | Mormon 8:36–37. Here, Moroni identifies some specific aspects of modern life that he's been able to glimpse in his vision of the future. He knows that when the Book of Mormon comes forth, it will be judged by a society that is prideful, rich, and corrupt. He particularly targets the love of money as the cancer that rots this society, which will neglect the poor. (Since the Book of Mormon came forth in a time when the United States was first emerging as a nation but one that would become the wealthiest country on earth, these seem prophetic words indeed.)

The Book of Mormon in the Modern World

34 Behold, the Lord hath shown unto me great and marvelous things concerning that which must shortly come, at that day when these things shall come forth among you.[7]

35 Behold, I speak unto you as if ye were present, and yet ye are not. But behold, Jesus Christ hath shown you unto me, and I know your doing.

36 And I know that ye do walk in the pride of your hearts; and there are none save a few only who do not lift themselves up in the pride of their hearts, unto the wearing of very fine apparel, unto envying, and strifes, and malice, and persecutions, and all manner of iniquities; and your churches, yea, even every one, have become polluted because of the pride of your hearts.

37 For behold, ye do love money, and your substance, and your fine apparel, and the adorning of your churches, more than ye love the poor and the needy, the sick and the afflicted.[8]

. . . . .

Mormon 9

The God of Miracles

. . . . .

8 Behold I say unto you, he that denieth these things knoweth not the gospel of Christ; yea, he has not read the scriptures; if so, he does not understand them.

9 For do we not read that God is the same yesterday, today, and forever, and in him there is no variableness neither shadow of changing?

9 Mormon 9:10–11. Moroni declares emphatically that since God is "the same yesterday, today and forever," then a willingness to perform miracles is still a foundational part of God's character. Mormons believe that the ancient prophet is here speaking to a modern culture that would be prone to denying miracles; if people aren't seeing miracles in the modern world, Moroni places the blame squarely on their own shoulders because they lack faith. Remember that the Book of Mormon came forth at the close of the Enlightenment, or Age of Reason, when many people believed that science and empirical knowledge could be depended upon to fully explain the workings of the universe. Seeing into the future, Moroni speaks to these people directly by proclaiming that the God of Abraham, Isaac, and Jacob is still a God of miracles. (Skeptics and critics of the Book of Mormon, of course, point to this same passage as evidence that Joseph Smith wrote the book, since it so clearly refers to the intellectual conflicts of the early nineteenth century.)

10 Mormon 9:27. This final exhortation could be termed "Moroni's creed" because it encapsulates the message that Moroni has been trying to convey all along: Readers should listen to God's words, pray in faith, and gradually work out their salvation through love and humility.

10 And now if ye have imagined up unto yourselves a god who doth vary, and in whom there is shadow of changing, then have ye imagined up unto yourselves a god who is not a God of miracles.

11 But behold, I will show unto you a God of miracles, even the God of Abraham, and the God of Isaac, and the God of Jacob; and it is that same God who created the heavens and the earth, and all things that in them are.[9]

. . . . .

20 And the reason why he ceaseth to do miracles among the children of men is because that they dwindle in unbelief, and depart from the right way, and know not the God in whom they should trust.

21 Behold, I say unto you that whoso believeth in Christ, doubting nothing, whatsoever he shall ask the Father in the name of Christ it shall be granted him; and this promise is unto all, even unto the ends of the earth.

. . . . .

Moroni's Creed

27 O then despise not, and wonder not, but hearken unto the words of the Lord, and ask the Father in the name of Jesus for what things soever ye shall stand in need. Doubt not, but be believing, and begin as in times of old, and come unto the Lord with all your heart, and work out your own salvation with fear and trembling before him.[10]

28 Be wise in the days of your probation; strip yourselves of all uncleanness; ask not, that ye may consume it on your lusts, but ask with a firmness unshaken, that ye will yield to no temptation, but that ye will serve the true and living God.

29 See that ye are not baptized unworthily; see that ye partake not of the sacrament of Christ unworthily; but see that ye do all things in

11 Mormon 9:30. Moroni's voice—as it is contained in the words of this book—seems to come from the grave; as he puts it, "I speak unto you as though I spake from the dead." He is speaking to the modern reader, but he has been dead for nearly sixteen hundred years. Incidentally, the 1981 edition reads, "you shall have my words," not "you shall hear my words."

12 Mormon 9:31. Again, Moroni admonishes readers that the record contains "imperfections" that they will be expected to transcend. These could include errors in translation or transmission, as well as the incomplete nature of the records he's already mentioned.

worthiness, and do it in the name of Jesus Christ, the Son of the living God; and if ye do this, and endure to the end, ye will in nowise be cast out.

30 Behold, I speak unto you as though I spake from the dead; for I know that ye shall hear my words.[11]

31 Condemn me not because of mine imperfection, neither my father, because of his imperfection, neither them who have written before him; but rather give thanks unto God that he hath made manifest unto you our imperfections, that ye may learn to be more wise than we have been.[12]

. . . . .

1 Moroni 7:1. Moroni decides to include some of the spiritual teachings of his father, Mormon, which he thinks will be most useful to the modern reader.

2 Moroni 7:9. Just as good works mean nothing if they stem from evil intentions or a grudging heart, people need to pray with "real intent" (a phrase Moroni and his father use several times), or their prayers will not be of any benefit to them. For example, if a woman prays to be able to forgive a person she really doesn't *want* to forgive, the prayer will "profit her nothing."

8 □ The Book of Moroni

True Prayer and the Gift of the Holy Ghost

Moroni 7

1 And now I, Moroni, write a few of the words of my father Mormon,[1] which he spake concerning faith, hope, and charity; for after this manner did he speak unto the people, as he taught them in the synagogue which they had built for the place of worship.

. . . . .

Good and Evil

6 For behold, God hath said a man being evil cannot do that which is good; for if he offereth a gift, or prayeth unto God, except he shall do it with real intent it profiteth him nothing.

7 For behold, it is not counted unto him for righteousness.

8 For behold, if a man being evil giveth a gift, he doeth it grudgingly; wherefore it is counted unto him the same as if he had retained the gift; wherefore he is counted evil before God.

9 And likewise also is it counted evil unto a man, if he shall pray and not with real intent of heart; yea, and it profiteth him nothing, for God receiveth none such.[2]

10 Wherefore, a man being evil cannot do that which is good; neither will he give a good gift.

. . . . .

219

3 | Moroni 7:13. The criterion for knowing if something is of God is to determine whether that thing invites a person—even *entices* a person—to do good and to serve God. Like the ancient prophet Alma, Moroni stresses the practical, experimental strategy of testing something out to see what its fruits will be. Everything that does entice a person to love, serve, and do good is inspired of God, plain and simple.

4 | Moroni 7:16–19. Mormons believe that the "spirit of Christ" or "light of Christ" is an inherent part of every human being's divine nature. The light of Christ functions much in the same way as a conscience, helping people discern good from evil and know which path to take. In addition to this guidance, baptized members of the LDS Church also receive through the laying on of hands a special blessing called the Gift of the Holy Ghost. Basically, this works like a personal Liahona, or spiritual compass, helping individual Latter-day Saints stay in tune with God's will and enjoy God's guidance in making decisions both large and small.

13 But behold, that which is of God inviteth and enticeth to do good continually; wherefore, every thing which inviteth and enticeth to do good, and to love God, and to serve him, is inspired of God.**3**

14 Wherefore, take heed, my beloved brethren, that ye do not judge that which is evil to be of God, or that which is good and of God to be of the devil.

15 For behold, my brethren, it is given unto you to judge, that ye may know good from evil; and the way to judge is as plain, that ye may know with a perfect knowledge, as the daylight is from the dark night.

16 For behold, the Spirit of Christ is given to every man,**4** that he may know good from evil; wherefore, I show unto you the way to judge; for every thing which inviteth to do good, and to persuade to believe in Christ, is sent forth by the power and gift of Christ; wherefore ye may know with a perfect knowledge it is of God.

. . . . .

19 Wherefore, I beseech of you, brethren, that ye should search diligently in the light of Christ that ye may know good from evil; and if ye will lay hold upon every good thing, and condemn it not, ye certainly will be a child of Christ.

20 And now, my brethren, how is it possible that ye can lay hold upon every good thing?

21 And now I come to that faith, of which I said I would speak; and I will tell you the way whereby ye may lay hold on every good thing.

. . . . .

Faith and Hope

25 Wherefore, by the ministering of angels, and by every word which proceeded forth out of the mouth of God, men began to exercise

5 Moroni 7:25–26. Mormon (as quoted by his son Moroni) teaches that faith is the instrument that allows people to "lay hold of every good thing."

6 Moroni 7:42. Mormon notes that faith and hope have a symbiotic relationship and go hand in hand. Hope is the state that first feeds the desire for faith and helps faith to grow (see Alma 32), but faith then nurtures hope by pointing to Christ's atonement, the resurrection, and eternal life.

7 Moroni 7:45–47. Compare chapter 13 of Paul's First Letter to the Corinthians in the New Testament, which in the King James version is almost identical to verse 45. Verse 46's promise that "charity never faileth" is the motto of the Relief Society, the worldwide women's organization of the LDS Church. Since 1842, the Relief Society's mission has been to provide aid and comfort to those in need, demonstrating the "pure love of Christ" through charitable work.

faith in Christ; and thus by faith, they did lay hold upon every good thing; and thus it was until the coming of Christ.

26 And after that he came men also were saved by faith in his name; and by faith, they become the sons of God. And as sure as Christ liveth he spake these words unto our fathers, saying: Whatsoever thing ye shall ask the Father in my name, which is good, in faith believing that ye shall receive, behold, it shall be done unto you.**5**

. . . . . .

40 And again, my beloved brethren, I would speak unto you concerning hope. How is it that ye can attain unto faith, save ye shall have hope?

41 And what is it that ye shall hope for? Behold I say unto you that ye shall have hope through the atonement of Christ and the power of his resurrection, to be raised unto life eternal, and this because of your faith in him according to the promise.

42 Wherefore, if a man have faith he must needs have hope; for without faith there cannot be any hope.**6**

43 And again, behold I say unto you that he cannot have faith and hope, save he shall be meek, and lowly of heart.

44 If so, his faith and hope is vain, for none is acceptable before God, save the meek and lowly in heart; and if a man be meek and lowly in heart, and confesses by the power of the Holy Ghost that Jesus is the Christ, he must needs have charity; for if he have not charity he is nothing; wherefore he must needs have charity.

45 And charity suffereth long, and is kind, and envieth not, and is not puffed up, seeketh not her own, is not easily provoked, thinketh no evil, and rejoiceth not in iniquity but rejoiceth in the truth, beareth all things, believeth all things, hopeth all things, endureth all things.**7**

8 Moroni 8:8. Mormon (as quoted by his son Moroni) explains one application of Christ's teaching that he came not to save the righteous but to save the sinners. Since small children are innocent in Christ and do not sin, they do not need to be baptized, because one of the primary purposes of baptism is to wash away sin. Mormons don't baptize children before the age of eight, which they believe is the age of accountability.

9 Moroni 8:9. Mormon teaches here that baptizing little children is not only redundant and of no spiritual value, but that it is actually insulting to God; it demonstrates a lack of trust that God will carry out his promise to care for the innocent.

46 Wherefore, my beloved brethren, if ye have not charity, ye are nothing, for charity never faileth. Wherefore, cleave unto charity, which is the greatest of all, for all things must fail—

47 But charity is the pure love of Christ, and it endureth forever; and whoso is found possessed of it at the last day, it shall be well with him.

48 Wherefore, my beloved brethren, pray unto the Father with all the energy of heart, that ye may be filled with this love, which he hath bestowed upon all who are true followers of his Son, Jesus Christ; that ye may become the sons of God; that when he shall appear we shall be like him, for we shall see him as he is; that we may have this hope; that we may be purified even as he is pure. Amen.

Baptism and the Age of Accountability

Moroni 8

. . . . .

8 Listen to the words of Christ, your Redeemer, your Lord and your God. Behold, I came into the world not to call the righteous but sinners to repentance; the whole need no physician, but they that are sick; wherefore, little children are whole, for they are not capable of committing sin; wherefore the curse of Adam is taken from them in me, that it hath no power over them; and the law of circumcision is done away in me.[8]

9 And after this manner did the Holy Ghost manifest the word of God unto me; wherefore, my beloved son, I know that it is solemn mockery before God, that ye should baptize little children.[9]

10 Behold I say unto you that this thing shall ye teach—repentance and baptism unto those who are accountable and capable of committing sin; yea, teach parents that they must repent and be

10 Moroni 8:12. Mormon uses even stronger language here to declare that little children are "alive in Christ"; not only are they without sin, but they are spiritually attuned and receptive to Christ. Mormon also opines that a God who condemns small children just because they had not been baptized would be a "partial" and "changeable" God, because so many babies and little children die without benefit of baptism.

baptized, and humble themselves as their little children, and they shall all be saved with their little children.

11 And their little children need no repentance, neither baptism. Behold, baptism is unto repentance to the fulfilling the commandments unto the remission of sins.

12 But little children are alive in Christ,[10] even from the foundation of the world; if not so, God is a partial God, and also a changeable God, and a respecter to persons; for how many little children have died without baptism!

13 Wherefore, if little children could not be saved without baptism, these must have gone to an endless hell.

14 Behold I say unto you, that he that supposeth that little children need baptism is in the gall of bitterness and in the bonds of iniquity, for he hath neither faith, hope, nor charity; wherefore, should he be cut off while in the thought, he must go down to hell.

15 For awful is the wickedness to suppose that God saveth one child because of baptism, and the other must perish because he hath no baptism.

16 Wo be unto them that shall pervert the ways of the Lord after this manner, for they shall perish except they repent. Behold, I speak with boldness, having authority from God; and I fear not what man can do; for perfect love casteth out all fear.

17 And I am filled with charity, which is everlasting love; wherefore, all children are alike unto me; wherefore, I love little children with a perfect love; and they are all alike and partakers of salvation.

. . . . .

11 Moroni 10:1. It's now about 421 CE, the close of the Book of Mormon and the end of Nephite civilization. Moroni, the last of the Nephites, seals up the records and offers a few final thoughts for the modern readers who will inherit the Book of Mormon many generations hence.

12 Moroni 10:4. This is one of the most quoted passages in the Book of Mormon, because missionaries ask "investigators" (those people who are learning about the LDS Church and thinking about converting) to read it and pray about it as they are making their spiritual decisions. Often referred to as "Moroni's challenge" or "Moroni's promise," it emphasizes the experiential and personal nature of prayer as a path to truth. Again, Moroni emphasizes the need for sincerity and "real intent" in prayer.

13 Moroni 10:30. Moroni's final words stress the need for the reader to "come unto Christ" (see also verse 32). This is the essential message of the entire Book of Mormon.

Receiving Spiritual Truth

Moroni 10

1 Now I, Moroni, write somewhat as seemeth me good; and I write unto my brethren, the Lamanites; and I would that they should know that more than four hundred and twenty years have passed away since the sign was given of the coming of Christ.**11**

2 And I seal up these records, after I have spoken a few words by way of exhortation unto you.

3 Behold, I would exhort you that when ye shall read these things, if it be wisdom in God that ye should read them, that ye would remember how merciful the Lord hath been unto the children of men, from the creation of Adam even down unto the time that ye shall receive these things, and ponder it in your hearts.

4 And when ye shall receive these things, I would exhort you that ye would ask God, the Eternal Father, in the name of Christ, if these things are not true; and if ye shall ask with a sincere heart, with real intent, having faith in Christ, he will manifest the truth of it unto you, by the power of the Holy Ghost.**12**

5 And by the power of the Holy Ghost ye may know the truth of all things.

6 And whatsoever thing is good is just and true; wherefore, nothing that is good denieth the Christ, but acknowledgeth that he is.

. . . . .

30 And again I would exhort you that ye would come unto Christ,**13** and lay hold upon every good gift, and touch not the evil gift, nor the unclean thing.

14 | Moroni 10:32–33. Moroni emphasizes the concert of human effort (denying "ungodliness," striving to love God wholly) and divine grace in the sanctification of the soul. Sanctification—the gradual process of becoming holy—is first made possible by God's grace and Christ's sacrifice, and then put into action by the receptive individual who opens himself or herself to the gift of grace.

15 | Moroni 10:34. Moroni, now dying, expects to be received into spirit paradise and there await the eventual resurrection at the last day. Interestingly, he didn't have to wait as long as the rest of us will. The LDS Church teaches that a few choice spirits have already been resurrected and have become angels, who have perfect, glorified bodies of flesh and bone. Moroni was one such individual, which gave him the means to visit Joseph Smith throughout the 1820s and carry God's message about the location and significance of the Book of Mormon. In homage to Moroni's role in ushering forth the restoration of the gospel, many LDS temples feature a statue of the Angel Moroni at the top of a spire. He is shown blowing a trumpet, which symbolizes his task in declaring the good news of Christ's love and resurrection. The Angel Moroni of the 1820s is the resurrected person who was in life Moroni, the final editor of the Book of Mormon and the last survivor of the Nephite people.

31 And awake, and arise from the dust, O Jerusalem; yea, and put on thy beautiful garments, O daughter of Zion; and strengthen thy stakes and enlarge thy borders forever, that thou mayest no more be confounded, that the covenants of the Eternal Father which he hath made unto thee, O house of Israel, may be fulfilled.

32 Yea, come unto Christ, and be perfected in him, and deny yourselves of all ungodliness; and if ye shall deny yourselves of all ungodliness and love God with all your might, mind and strength, then is his grace sufficient for you, that by his grace ye may be perfect in Christ; and if by the grace of God ye are perfect in Christ, ye can in nowise deny the power of God.[14]

33 And again, if ye by the grace of God are perfect in Christ, and deny not his power, then are ye sanctified in Christ by the grace of God, through the shedding of the blood of Christ, which is in the covenant of the Father unto the remission of your sins, that ye become holy, without spot.

34 And now I bid unto all, farewell. I soon go to rest in the paradise of God, until my spirit and body shall again reunite, and I am brought forth triumphant through the air, to meet you before the pleasing bar of the great Jehovah, the Eternal Judge of both quick and dead. Amen.[15]

☐ Notes

Notes to Introduction

1. Noel B. Reynolds, "The Coming Forth of the Book of Mormon in the Twentieth Century," in *Dialogue: A Journal of Mormon Thought* 38, no. 2 (1999): 8.
2. Grant Underwood, "Book of Mormon Usage in Early LDS Theology," in *Dialogue: A Journal of Mormon Thought* 17 (Autumn 1984), 39, 41. The passage cited most often was Ether 13:4–8, which speaks of a "New Jerusalem upon this land."
3. Kenneth L. Woodward, "A Mormon Moment," *Newsweek* (September 10, 2001), 44.
4. "The Coming Forth of the Book of Mormon," in *Book of Mormon Reference Companion* (Salt Lake City: Deseret Book Company, 2003), 9.
5. For a full account of the translation of the Book of Mormon, see the first two chapters of Terryl Givens, *By the Hand of Mormon: The American Scripture That Launched a New World Religion* (New York: Oxford University Press, 2002).
6. Richard Dilworth Rust and Donald W. Parry, "Book of Mormon Literature" in *Encyclopedia of Mormonism*, online at www.lightplanet.com/mormons/basic/bom/literature_eom.htm.

Notes to Chapter 1

39. "another kind of quadruped": See, for example, "Once More: The Horse," in *Re-Exploring the Book of Mormon: A Decade of New Research,* edited by John Welch (Salt Lake City: Deseret Book Company, 1992), 98–100.

Notes to Chapter 2

11. "poetic rendering": Grant Hardy, *The Book of Mormon: A Reader's Edition* (Urbana: University of Illinois, 2003), 71–74.
15. Nephi's anger: Catherine Thomas, "A Great Deliverance," in *Studies in Scripture, Volume 7: 1 Nephi to Alma 29,* edited by Kent P. Jackson (Salt Lake City: Deseret Book Company, 1987), 108.

Notes to Chapter 3

24. God's character as revealed in the allegory of the olive tree: Jeffrey R. Holland, "The Grandeur of God," *Ensign* (November 2003), 71.

Notes to Chapter 4

6. The merits of Christ: Joseph Fielding Smith, *Improvement Era* (June 1966), 538.

Notes to Chapter 5

7. "Countenance": Andrew C. Skinner, "Alma's 'Pure Testimony,'" in *Studies in Scripture, Volume 7: 1 Nephi to Alma 29*, edited by Kent P. Jackson (Salt Lake City: Deseret Book Company, 1987), 301.

17. "Who is Satan?": Elder John Taylor, quoted in Rulon T. Burton, *We Believe: Doctrines and Principles of The Church of Jesus Christ of Latter-day Saints* (Salt Lake City: Tabernacle Books, 1994), 213.

21. Alma 32, faith, and hope: Eugene England, *Why the Church Is as True as the Gospel*, summarized by Kerry Shirts at www2.ida.net/graphics/shirtail/excerpts.htm.

22. "Faith must precede certitude": Rodney Turner, "A Faith unto Salvation," in *Studies in Scripture, Volume 8: Alma 30 to Moroni* (Salt Lake City: Deseret Book, 1988), 22.

32. Alma 36 chiasm: John W. Welch and J. Gregory Welch, *Charting the Book of Mormon: Visual Aids for Personal Study and Teaching* (Provo, Utah: FARMS, 1999), chart 132.

Notes to Chapter 6

6. "The wounded Christ": Jeffrey R. Holland, "Thoughts on Gospel Doctrine Lesson 37," at http://deseretbook.com/mormon-life/curric.

17. Healing in 3 Nephi: Krister Stendahl, "The Sermon on the Mount and Third Nephi," in *Reflections on Mormonism: Judeo-Christian Parallels*, edited by Truman G. Madsen (Provo, Utah: The Religious Studies Center, 1978).

Notes to Chapter 7

3. "Mormon's lamentation": Grant Hardy, *The Book of Mormon: A Reader's Edition* (Urbana: University of Illinois, 2003), 566–67.

☐ Suggested Readings

Benson, Ezra Taft. *A Witness and a Warning: A Modern-day Prophet Testifies of the Book of Mormon.* Salt Lake City: Deseret Book Company, 1988.

Bushman, Claudia Lauper, and Richard Bushman. *Building the Kingdom: A History of Mormons in America.* New York: Oxford University Press, 2001.

Bushman, Richard. *Joseph Smith and the Beginnings of Mormonism.* Urbana: University of Illinois Press, 1984.

Givens, Terryl. *By the Hand of Mormon: The American Scripture That Launched a New World Religion.* New York: Oxford University Press, 2002.

Hardy, Grant. *The Book of Mormon: A Reader's Edition.* Urbana: University of Illinois Press, 2003.

Largey, Dennis L., general editor. *Book of Mormon Reference Companion.* Salt Lake City: Deseret Book, 2003.

Millet, Robert L. *A Different Jesus?: The Christ of the Latter-day Saints.* Grand Rapids, Mich.: Eerdmans, 2005.

Ostling, Richard, and Joan K. Ostling. *Mormon America: The Power and the Promise.* San Francisco: HarperSanFrancisco, 1999.

Riess, Jana, and Christopher Kimball Bigelow. *Mormonism for Dummies.* Indianapolis: Wiley Publishing, 2005.

Shipps, Jan. *Mormonism: The Story of a New Religious Tradition.* Urbana: University of Illinois Press, 1985.

Welch, John W., and J. Gregory Welch. *Charting the Book of Mormon: Visual Aids for Personal Study and Teaching.* Provo, Utah: FARMS, 1999.

Notes

Global Spiritual Perspectives

Spiritual Perspectives on America's Role as Superpower
by the Editors at SkyLight Paths

Are we the world's good neighbor or a global bully? Explores broader issues surrounding the use of American power around the world, including in Iraq and the Middle East. From a spiritual perspective, what are America's responsibilities as the only remaining superpower? Contributors:

Dr. Beatrice Bruteau • Rev. Dr. Joan Brown Campbell • Tony Campolo • Rev. Forrest Church • Lama Surya Das • Matthew Fox • Kabir Helminski • Thich Nhat Hanh • Eboo Patel • Abbot M. Basil Pennington, ocso • Dennis Prager • Rosemary Radford Ruether • Wayne Teasdale • Rev. William McD. Tully • Rabbi Arthur Waskow • John Wilson

5½ x 8½, 256 pp, Quality PB, ISBN 1-893361-81-0 **$16.95**

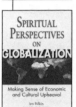

Spiritual Perspectives on Globalization, 2nd Edition
Making Sense of Economic and Cultural Upheaval
by Ira Rifkin; Foreword by Dr. David Little, Harvard Divinity School

What is globalization? What are spiritually minded people saying and doing about it? This lucid introduction surveys the religious landscape, explaining in clear and nonjudgmental language the beliefs that motivate spiritual leaders, activists, theologians, academics, and others involved on all sides of the issue. This edition includes a new Afterword and Discussion Guide designed for group use.

5½ x 8½, 256 pp, Quality PB, ISBN 1-59473-045-8 **$16.99**

Hinduism / Vedanta

Meditation & Its Practices: A Definitive Guide to Techniques and Traditions of Meditation in Yoga and Vedanta
by Swami Adiswarananda

The complete sourcebook for exploring Hinduism's two most time-honored traditions of meditation. Drawing on both classic and contemporary sources, this comprehensive sourcebook outlines the scientific, psychological, and spiritual elements of Yoga and Vedanta meditation.

6 x 9, 504 pp, HC, ISBN 1-893361-83-7 **$34.95**

Sri Sarada Devi: Her Teachings and Conversations
Translated and with Notes by Swami Nikhilananda
Edited and with an Introduction by Swami Adiswarananda

Brings to life the Holy Mother's teachings on human affliction, self-control, and peace in ways both personal and profound, and illuminates her role as the power, scripture, joy, and guiding spirit of the Ramakrishna Order.

6 x 9, 288 pp, HC, ISBN 1-59473-070-9 **$29.99**

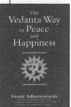

The Vedanta Way to Peace and Happiness
by Swami Adiswarananda

Using language that is accessible to people of all faiths and backgrounds, this book introduces the timeless teachings of Vedanta—divinity of the individual soul, unity of all existence, and oneness with the Divine—ancient wisdom as relevant to human happiness today as it was thousands of years ago.

6 x 9, 240 pp, HC, ISBN 1-59473-034-2 **$29.99**

Children's Spirituality

Because Nothing Looks Like God
by Lawrence and Karen Kushner; Full-color illus. by Dawn W. Majewski
Real-life examples of happiness and sadness—from goodnight stories, to the hope and fear felt the first time at bat, to the closing moments of life—introduce children to the possibilities of spiritual life.
11 x 8½, 32 pp, HC, Full-color illus., ISBN 1-58023-092-X **$16.95**
For ages 4 & up (a Jewish Lights book)
Also available:
Teacher's Guide, 8½ x 11, 22 pp, PB, ISBN 1-58023-140-3 **$6.95** *For ages 5–8*

Becoming Me: A Story of Creation
by Martin Boroson; Full-color illus. by Christopher Gilvan-Cartwright
Told in the personal "voice" of the Creator, here is a story about creation and relationship that is about each one of us.
8 x 10, 32 pp, Full-color illus., HC, ISBN 1-893361-11-X **$16.95** *For ages 4 & up*

But God Remembered: Stories of Women from Creation to the Promised Land
by Sandy Eisenberg Sasso; Full-color illus. by Bethanne Andersen
A fascinating collection of four different stories of women only briefly mentioned in biblical tradition and religious texts; all teach important values through their actions and faith. 9 x 12, 32 pp, HC, Full-color illus., ISBN 1-879045-43-5 **$16.95**
For ages 8 & up (a Jewish Lights book)

Cain & Abel: Finding the Fruits of Peace
by Sandy Eisenberg Sasso; Full-color illus. by Joani Keller Rothenberg
A sensitive recasting of the ancient tale shows we have the power to deal with anger in positive ways. Provides questions for kids and adults to explore together. "Editor's Choice"—American Library Association's *Booklist*
9 x 12, 32 pp, HC, Full-color illus., ISBN 1-58023-123-3 **$16.95** *For ages 5 & up (a Jewish Lights book)*

Does God Hear My Prayer?
by August Gold; Full-color photo illus. by Diane Hardy Waller
This colorful book introduces preschoolers as well as young readers to prayer and how prayer can help them express their own fears, wants, sadness, surprise, and joy. 10 x 8½, 32 pp, Quality PB, Full-color photo illus., ISBN 1-59473-102-0 **$8.99**

The 11th Commandment: Wisdom from Our Children
by The Children of America
"If there were an Eleventh Commandment, what would it be?" Children of many religious denominations across America answer this question—in their own drawings and words. "A rare book of spiritual celebration for all people, of all ages, for all time." —*Bookviews*
8 x 10, 48 pp, HC, Full-color illus., ISBN 1-879045-46-X **$16.95** *For ages 4 & up (a Jewish Lights book)*

For Heaven's Sake
by Sandy Eisenberg Sasso; Full-color illus. by Kathryn Kunz Finney
Everyone talked about heaven: "Thank heavens." "Heaven forbid." "For heaven's sake, Isaiah." But no one would say what heaven was or how to find it. So Isaiah decides to find out, by seeking answers from many different people.
9 x 12, 32 pp, HC, Full-color illus., ISBN 1-58023-054-7 **$16.95** *For ages 4 & up (a Jewish Lights book)*

God in Between
by Sandy Eisenberg Sasso; Full-color illus. by Sally Sweetland
If you wanted to find God, where would you look? A magical, mythical tale that teaches that God can be found where we are: within all of us and the relationships between us. 9 x 12, 32 pp, HC, Full-color illus., ISBN 1-879045-86-9 **$16.95**
For ages 4 & up (a Jewish Lights book)

Children's Spirituality

God Said Amen
by Sandy Eisenberg Sasso; Full-color illus. by Avi Katz
A warm and inspiring tale of two kingdoms that shows us that we need only reach out to each other to find the answers to our prayers.
9 x 12, 32 pp, HC, Full-color illus., ISBN 1-58023-080-6 **$16.95**
For ages 4 & up (a Jewish Lights book)

How Does God Listen?
by Kay Lindahl; Full-color photo illus. by Cynthia Maloney
How do we know when God is listening to us? Children will find the answers to these questions as they engage their senses while the story unfolds, learning how God listens in the wind, waves, clouds, hot chocolate, perfume, our tears and our laughter.
10 x 8½, 32 pp, Quality PB, Full-color photo illus., ISBN 1-59473-084-9 **$8.99**
For ages 3–6

In God's Name
by Sandy Eisenberg Sasso; Full-color illus. by Phoebe Stone
Like an ancient myth in its poetic text and vibrant illustrations, this award-winning modern fable about the search for God's name celebrates the diversity and, at the same time, the unity of all the people of the world.
9 x 12, 32 pp, HC, Full-color illus., ISBN 1-879045-26-5 **$16.95**
For ages 4 & up (a Jewish Lights book)

Also available in Spanish:
El nombre de Dios
9 x 12, 32 pp, HC, Full-color illus., ISBN 1-893361-63-2 **$16.95**

Where Does God Live?
by August Gold; Full-color photo illus. by Matthew J. Perlman
Using simple, everyday examples that children can relate to, this colorful book helps young readers develop a personal understanding of God.
10 x 8½, 32 pp, Quality PB, Full-color photo illus., ISBN 1-893361-39-X **$8.99**
For ages 3–6

In Our Image: God's First Creatures
by Nancy Sohn Swartz; Full-color illus. by Melanie Hall
A playful new twist on the Creation story—from the perspective of the animals. Celebrates the interconnectedness of nature and the harmony of all living things. 9 x 12, 32 pp, HC, Full-color illus., ISBN 1-879045-99-0 **$16.95**
For ages 4 & up (a Jewish Lights book)

Noah's Wife: The Story of Naamah
by Sandy Eisenberg Sasso; Full-color illus. by Bethanne Andersen
This new story, based on an ancient text, opens readers' religious imaginations to new ideas about the well-known story of the Flood. When God tells Noah to bring the animals of the world onto the ark, God also calls on Naamah, Noah's wife, to save each plant on Earth.
9 x 12, 32 pp, HC, Full-color illus., ISBN 1-58023-134-9 **$16.95**
For ages 4 & up (a Jewish Lights book)

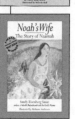

Also available:
Naamah: Noah's Wife (A Board Book)
by Sandy Eisenberg Sasso, Full-color illus by Bethanne Andersen
5 x 5, 24 pp, Board Book, Full-color illus., ISBN 1-893361-56-X **$7.99** *For ages 0–4*

Children's Spirituality—Board Books

How Did the Animals Help God? (A Board Book)
by Nancy Sohn Swartz, Full-color illus. by Melanie Hall
Abridged from Nancy Sohn Swartz's *In Our Image*, God asks all of nature to offer gifts to humankind—with a promise that they will care for creation in return.
5 x 5, 24 pp, Board Book, Full-color illus., ISBN 1-59473-044-X **$7.99** *For ages 0–4*

Where Is God? (A Board Book)
by Lawrence and Karen Kushner; Full-color illus. by Dawn W. Majewski
A gentle way for young children to explore how God is with us every day, in every way. Abridged from *Because Nothing Looks Like God* by Lawrence and Karen Kushner.   5 x 5, 24 pp, Board, Full-color illus., ISBN 1-893361-17-9 **$7.99** *For ages 0–4*

What Does God Look Like? (A Board Book)
by Lawrence and Karen Kushner; Full-color illus. by Dawn W. Majewski
A simple way for young children to explore the ways that we "see" God. Abridged from *Because Nothing Looks Like God* by Lawrence and Karen Kushner.
5 x 5, 24 pp, Board, Full-color illus., ISBN 1-893361-23-3 **$7.95** *For ages 0–4*

How Does God Make Things Happen? (A Board Book)
by Lawrence and Karen Kushner; Full-color illus. by Dawn W. Majewski
A charming invitation for young children to explore how God makes things happen in our world. Abridged from *Because Nothing Looks Like God* by Lawrence and Karen Kushner.   5 x 5, 24 pp, Board, Full-color illus., ISBN 1-893361-24-1 **$7.95** *For ages 0–4*

What Is God's Name? (A Board Book)
by Sandy Eisenberg Sasso; Full-color illus. by Phoebe Stone
Everyone and everything in the world has a name. What is God's name? Abridged from the award-winning *In God's Name* by Sandy Eisenberg Sasso.
5 x 5, 24 pp, Board, Full-color illus., ISBN 1-893361-10-1 **$7.99** *For ages 0–4*

What You Will See Inside ...

This important new series of books is designed to show children ages 6–10 the Who, What, When, Where, Why and How of traditional houses of worship, liturgical celebrations, and rituals of different world faiths, empowering them to respect and understand their own religious traditions—and those of their friends and neighbors.

What You Will See Inside a Catholic Church
by Reverend Michael Keane; Foreword by Robert J. Keeley, Ed.D.
Full-color photographs by Aaron Pepis
A colorful, fun-to-read introduction to the traditions of Catholic worship and faith. Visually explains the common use of the altar, processional cross, baptismal font, votive candles, and more.   8½ x 10½, 32 pp, HC, ISBN 1-893361-54-3 **$17.95**

Also available in Spanish: **Lo que se puede ver dentro de una iglesia católica**
8½ x 10¼, 32 pp, Full-color photos, HC, ISBN 1-893361-66-7 **$16.95**

What You Will See Inside a Mosque
by Aisha Karen Khan; Photographs by Aaron Pepis
Featuring full-page pictures and concise descriptions of what is happening, the objects used, the spiritual leaders and laypeople who have specific roles, and the spiritual intent of the believers. Demystifies the celebrations and ceremonies of Islam throughout the year.
8½ x 10½, 32 pp, Full-color photos, HC, ISBN 1-893361-60-8 **$16.95**

What You Will See Inside a Synagogue
by Rabbi Lawrence A. Hoffman and Dr. Ron Wolfson; Full-color photos by Bill Aron
A colorful, fun-to-read introduction that explains the ways and whys of Jewish worship and religious life. Full-page photos; concise but informative descriptions of the objects used, the clergy and laypeople who have specific roles, and much more.
8½ x 10½, 32 pp, Full-color photos, HC, ISBN 1-59473-012-1 **$17.99**

Children's Spiritual Biography

Ten Amazing People
And How They Changed the World
by Maura D. Shaw; Foreword by Dr. Robert Coles
Full-color illus. by Stephen Marchesi

For ages 7 & up

Black Elk • Dorothy Day • Malcolm X • Mahatma Gandhi • Martin Luther King, Jr. • Mother Teresa • Janusz Korczak • Desmond Tutu • Thich Nhat Hanh • Albert Schweitzer

This vivid, inspirational, and authoritative book will open new possibilities for children by telling the stories of how ten of the past century's greatest leaders changed the world in important ways.

8½ x 11, 48 pp, HC, Full-color illus., ISBN 1-893361-47-0 **$17.95** *For ages 7 & up*

Spiritual Biographies for Young People—For ages 7 and up

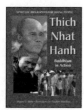
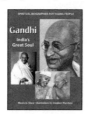

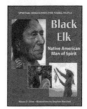

Black Elk: Native American Man of Spirit
by Maura D. Shaw; Full-color illus. by Stephen Marchesi
Through historically accurate illustrations and photos, inspiring age-appropriate activities, and Black Elk's own words, this colorful biography introduces children to a remarkable person who ensured that the traditions and beliefs of his people would not be forgotten.
6¾ x 8¾, 32 pp, HC, Full-color illus., ISBN 1-59473-043-1 **$12.99**

Dorothy Day: A Catholic Life of Action
by Maura D. Shaw; Full-color illus. by Stephen Marchesi
Introduces children to one of the most inspiring women of the twentieth century, a down-to-earth spiritual leader who saw the presence of God in every person she met. Includes practical activities, a timeline, and a list of important words to know.
6¾ x 8¾, 32 pp, HC, Full-color illus., ISBN 1-59473-011-3 **$12.99**

Gandhi: India's Great Soul
by Maura D. Shaw; Full-color illus. by Stephen Marchesi
There are a number of biographies of Gandhi written for young readers, but this is the only one that balances a simple text with illustrations, photographs, and activities that encourage children and adults to talk about how to make changes happen without violence. Introduces children to important concepts of freedom, equality, and justice among people of all backgrounds and religions.
6¾ x 8¾, 32 pp, HC, Full-color illus., ISBN 1-893361-91-8 **$12.95**

Thich Nhat Hanh: Buddhism in Action
by Maura D. Shaw; Full-color illus. by Stephen Marchesi
Warm illustrations, photos, age-appropriate activities, and Thich Nhat Hanh's own poems introduce a great man to children in a way they can understand and enjoy. Includes a list of important Buddhist words to know.
6¾ x 8¾, 32 pp, HC, Full-color illus., ISBN 1-893361-87-X **$12.95**

Kabbalah from Jewish Lights Publishing

Ehyeh: A Kabbalah for Tomorrow *by Dr. Arthur Green*
6 x 9, 224 pp, Quality PB, ISBN 1-58023-213-2 **$16.99**; HC, ISBN 1-58023-125-X **$21.95**

The Enneagram and Kabbalah: Reading Your Soul *by Rabbi Howard A. Addison*
6 x 9, 176 pp, Quality PB, ISBN 1-58023-001-6 **$15.95**

Finding Joy: A Practical Spiritual Guide to Happiness *by Dannel I. Schwartz with Mark Hass*
6 x 9, 192 pp, Quality PB, ISBN 1-58023-009-1 **$14.95**; HC, ISBN 1-879045-53-2 **$19.95**

The Gift of Kabbalah: Discovering the Secrets of Heaven, Renewing Your Life on Earth
by Tamar Frankiel, Ph.D.
6 x 9, 256 pp, Quality PB, ISBN 1-58023-141-1 **$16.95**; HC, ISBN 1-58023-108-X **$21.95**

Zohar: Annotated & Explained
Translation and annotation by Dr. Daniel C. Matt. Foreword by Andrew Harvey
5½ x 8½, 160 pp, Quality PB, ISBN 1-893361-51-9 **$15.99**

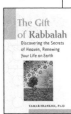

Meditation / Prayer

Prayers to an Evolutionary God
by William Cleary; Afterword by Diarmuid O'Murchu
How is it possible to pray when God is dislocated from heaven, dispersed all around us, and more of a creative force than an all-knowing father? Inspired by the spiritual and scientific teachings of Diarmuid O'Murchu and Teilhard de Chardin, Cleary reveals that religion and science can be combined to create an expanding view of the universe—an evolutionary faith.
6 x 9, 208 pp, HC, ISBN 1-59473-006-7 **$21.99**

The Song of Songs: A Spiritual Commentary
by M. Basil Pennington, OCSO; Illustrations by Phillip Ratner
Join M. Basil Pennington as he ruminates on the Bible's most challenging mystical text. You will follow a path into the Songs that weaves through his inspired words and the evocative drawings of Jewish artist Phillip Ratner—a path that reveals your own humanity and leads to the deepest delight of your soul.
6 x 9, 160 pp, HC, 14 b/w illus., ISBN 1-59473-004-0 **$19.99**

Women of Color Pray: Voices of Strength, Faith, Healing, Hope, and Courage
Edited and with Introductions by Christal M. Jackson
Through these prayers, poetry, lyrics, meditations and affirmations, you will share in the strong and undeniable connection women of color share with God. It will challenge you to explore new ways of prayerful expression.
5 x 7¼, 208 pp, Quality PB, ISBN 1-59473-077-6 **$15.99**

The Art of Public Prayer, 2nd Edition: Not for Clergy Only
by Lawrence A. Hoffman 6 x 9, 288 pp, Quality PB, ISBN 1-893361-06-3 **$18.95**

Finding Grace at the Center: The Beginning of Centering Prayer
by M. Basil Pennington, ocso, Thomas Keating, ocso, and Thomas E. Clarke, SJ
5 x 7¼, 112 pp, HC, ISBN 1-893361-69-1 **$14.95**

A Heart of Stillness: A Complete Guide to Learning the Art of Meditation
by David A. Cooper 5½ x 8½, 272 pp, Quality PB, ISBN 1-893361-03-9 **$16.95**

Meditation without Gurus: A Guide to the Heart of Practice
by Clark Strand 5½ x 8½, 192 pp, Quality PB, ISBN 1-893361-93-4 **$16.95**

Praying with Our Hands: Twenty-One Practices of Embodied Prayer from the
World's Spiritual Traditions *by Jon M. Sweeney; Photographs by Jennifer J. Wilson; Foreword by
Mother Tessa Bielecki; Afterword by Taitetsu Unno, PhD*
8 x 8, 96 pp, 22 duotone photographs, Quality PB, ISBN 1-893361-16-0 **$16.95**

Silence, Simplicity & Solitude: A Complete Guide to Spiritual Retreat at Home
by David A. Cooper 5½ x 8½, 336 pp, Quality PB, ISBN 1-893361-04-7 **$16.95**

Three Gates to Meditation Practice: A Personal Journey into Sufism, Buddhism,
and Judaism *by David A. Cooper* 5½ x 8½, 240 pp, Quality PB, ISBN 1-893361-22-5 **$16.95**

Women Pray: Voices through the Ages, from Many Faiths, Cultures, and Traditions
Edited and with introductions by Monica Furlong
5 x 7¼, 256 pp, Quality PB, ISBN 1-59473-071-7 **$15.99**;
Deluxe HC with ribbon marker, ISBN 1-893361-25-X **$19.95**

Midrash Fiction

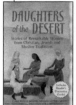

Daughters of the Desert: Tales of Remarkable Women from Christian, Jewish, and Muslim Traditions   *by Claire Rudolf Murphy, Meghan Nuttall Sayres, Mary Cronk Farrell, Sarah Conover, and Betsy Wharton*

Breathes new life into the old tales of our female ancestors in faith. Uses traditional scriptural passages as starting points, then with vivid detail fills in historical context and place. Chapters reveal the voices of Sarah, Hagar, Huldah, Esther, Salome, Mary Magdalene, Lydia, Khadija, Fatima, and many more. Historical fiction ideal for readers of all ages. Quality paperback includes reader's discussion guide.

5½ x 8½, 208 pp, Quality PB, ISBN 1-59473-106-3 **$14.99**; HC, 192 pp, ISBN 1-893361-72-1 **$19.95**

The Triumph of Eve & Other Subversive Bible Tales
by Matt Biers-Ariel
Many people were taught and remember only a one-dimensional Bible. These engaging retellings are the antidote to this—they're witty, often hilarious, always profound, and invite you to grapple with questions and issues that are often hidden in the original text.
5½ x 8½, 192 pp, HC, ISBN 1-59473-040-7 **$19.99**

Religious Etiquette / Reference

How to Be a Perfect Stranger, 3rd Edition: The Essential Religious Etiquette Handbook   *Edited by Stuart M. Matlins and Arthur J. Magida*
The indispensable guidebook to help the well-meaning guest when visiting other people's religious ceremonies. A straightforward guide to the rituals and celebrations of the major religions and denominations in the United States and Canada from the perspective of an interested guest of any other faith, based on information obtained from authorities of each religion. Belongs in every living room, library, and office. Covers:

African American Methodist Churches • Assemblies of God • Baha'i • Baptist • Buddhist • Christian Church (Disciples of Christ) • Christian Science (Church of Christ, Scientist) • Churches of Christ • Episcopalian and Anglican • Hindu • Islam • Jehovah's Witnesses • Jewish • Lutheran • Mennonite/Amish • Methodist • Mormon (Church of Jesus Christ of Latter-day Saints) • Native American/First Nations • Orthodox Churches • Pentecostal Church of God • Presbyterian • Quaker (Religious Society of Friends) • Reformed Church in America/Canada • Roman Catholic • Seventh-day Adventist • Sikh • Unitarian Universalist • United Church of Canada • United Church of Christ
6 x 9, 432 pp, Quality PB, ISBN 1-893361-67-5 **$19.95**

The Perfect Stranger's Guide to Funerals and Grieving Practices: A Guide to Etiquette in Other People's Religious Ceremonies   *Edited by Stuart M. Matlins*
6 x 9, 240 pp, Quality PB, ISBN 1-893361-20-9 **$16.95**

The Perfect Stranger's Guide to Wedding Ceremonies: A Guide to Etiquette in Other People's Religious Ceremonies   *Edited by Stuart M. Matlins*
6 x 9, 208 pp, Quality PB, ISBN 1-893361-19-5 **$16.95**

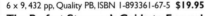

Spiritual Practice

Divining the Body
Reclaim the Holiness of Your Physical Self   *by Jan Phillips*
A practical and inspiring guidebook for connecting the body and soul in spiritual practice. Leads you into a milieu of reverence, mystery, and delight, helping you discover a redeemed sense of self.
8 x 8, 256 pp, Quality PB, ISBN 1-59473-080-6 **$16.99**

Finding Time for the Timeless
Spirituality in the Workweek   *by John McQuiston II*
Simple, refreshing stories that provide you with examples of how you can refocus and enrich your daily life using prayer or meditation, ritual, and other forms of spiritual practice.   5½ x 6½, 208 pp, HC, ISBN 1-59473-035-0 **$17.99**

The Gospel of Thomas: A Guidebook for Spiritual Practice
by Ron Miller; Translations by Stevan Davies
An innovative guide to bring a new spiritual classic into daily life. Offers a way to translate the wisdom of the Gospel of Thomas into daily practice, manifesting in your life the same consciousness revealed in Jesus of Nazareth. Written for readers of all religious backgrounds, this guidebook will help you to apply Jesus's wisdom to your own life and to the world around you.
6 x 9, 160 pp, Quality PB, ISBN 1-59473-047-4 **$14.99**

The Knitting Way: A Guide to Spiritual Self-Discovery
by Linda Skolnik and Janice MacDaniels
Through sharing stories, hands-on explorations, and daily cultivation, Skolnik and MacDaniels help you see beyond the surface of a simple craft in order to discover ways in which nuances of knitting can apply to the larger scheme of life and spirituality. Includes original knitting patterns.
7 x 9, 240 pp, Quality PB, ISBN 1-59473-079-2 **$16.99**

Earth, Water, Fire, and Air: Essential Ways of Connecting to Spirit
by Cait Johnson   6 x 9, 224 pp, HC, ISBN 1-893361-65-9 **$19.95**

Forty Days to Begin a Spiritual Life
Today's Most Inspiring Teachers Help You on Your Way
Edited by Maura Shaw and the Editors at SkyLight Paths; Foreword by Dan Wakefield
7 x 9, 144 pp, Quality PB, ISBN 1-893361-48-9 **$16.95**

Labyrinths from the Outside In
Walking to Spiritual Insight—A Beginner's Guide
by Donna Schaper and Carole Ann Camp
6 x 9, 208 pp, b/w illus. and photographs, Quality PB, ISBN 1-893361-18-7 **$16.95**

Practicing the Sacred Art of Listening: A Guide to Enrich Your Relationships
and Kindle Your Spiritual Life—The Listening Center Workshop
by Kay Lindahl   8 x 8, 176 pp, Quality PB, ISBN 1-893361-85-3 **$16.95**

The Sacred Art of Bowing: Preparing to Practice
by Andi Young   5½ x 8½, 128 pp, b/w illus., Quality PB, ISBN 1-893361-82-9 **$14.95**

The Sacred Art of Chant: Preparing to Practice
by Ana Hernandez   5½ x 8½, 192 pp, Quality PB, ISBN 1-59473-036-9 **$15.99**

The Sacred Art of Fasting: Preparing to Practice
by Thomas Ryan, CSP   5½ x 8½, 192 pp, Quality PB, ISBN 1-59473-078-4 **$15.99**

The Sacred Art of Listening: Forty Reflections for Cultivating a Spiritual Practice
by Kay Lindahl; Illustrations by Amy Schnapper
8 x 8, 160 pp, Illus., Quality PB, ISBN 1-893361-44-6 **$16.99**

Sacred Speech: A Practical Guide for Keeping Spirit in Your Speech
by Rev. Donna Schaper   6 x 9, 176 pp, Quality PB, ISBN 1-59473-068-7 **$15.99**;
HC, ISBN 1-893361-74-8 **$21.95**

Spirituality

Prayer for People Who Think Too Much
A Guide to Everyday, Anywhere Prayer from the World's Faith Traditions   *by Mitch Finley*
5½ x 8½, 224 pp, Quality PB, ISBN 1-893361-21-7 **$16.95**; HC, ISBN 1-893361-00-4 **$21.95**

The Shaman's Quest: Journeys in an Ancient Spiritual Practice
by Nevill Drury; with a Basic Introduction to Shamanism by Tom Cowan
5½ x 8½, 208 pp, Quality PB, ISBN 1-893361-68-3 **$16.95**

Show Me Your Way: The Complete Guide to Exploring Interfaith Spiritual Direction
by Howard A. Addison   5½ x 8½, 240 pp, Quality PB, ISBN 1-89336-41-1 **$16.95**;
HC, ISBN 1-893361-12-8 **$21.95**

Spirituality 101: The Indispensable Guide to Keeping—or Finding—Your Spiritual Life
on Campus   *by Harriet L. Schwartz, with contributions from college students at nearly thirty campuses across the United States*   6 x 9, 272 pp, Quality PB, ISBN 1-59473-000-8 **$16.99**

Spiritually Incorrect: Finding God in All the Wrong Places
by Dan Wakefield; Illus. by Marian DelVecchio
5½ x 8½, 192 pp, b/w illus., HC, ISBN 1-893361-88-8 **$21.95**

Spiritual Manifestos: Visions for Renewed Religious Life in America from Young
Spiritual Leaders of Many Faiths   *Edited by Niles Elliot Goldstein; Preface by Martin E. Marty*
6 x 9, 256 pp, HC, ISBN 1-893361-09-8 **$21.95**

A Walk with Four Spiritual Guides: Krishna, Buddha, Jesus, and Ramakrishna
by Andrew Harvey   5½ x 8½, 192 pp, 10 b/w photos & illus., HC, ISBN 1-893361-73-X **$21.95**

What Matters: Spiritual Nourishment for Head and Heart
by Frederick Franck   5 x 7¼, 144 pp, 50+ b/w illus., HC, ISBN 1-59473-013-X **$16.99**

Who Is My God?, 2nd Edition
An Innovative Guide to Finding Your Spiritual Identity
Created by the Editors at SkyLight Paths   6 x 9, 160 pp, Quality PB, ISBN 1-59473-014-8 **$15.99**

Spirituality—A Week Inside

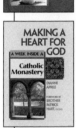

Come and Sit: A Week Inside Meditation Centers
by Marcia Z. Nelson; Foreword by Wayne Teasdale
The insider's guide to meditation in a variety of different spiritual traditions.
Traveling through Buddhist, Hindu, Christian, Jewish, and Sufi traditions, this essential guide takes you to different meditation centers to meet the teachers and students and learn about the practices, demystifying the meditation experience.
6 x 9, 224 pp, b/w photographs, Quality PB, ISBN 1-893361-35-7 **$16.95**

Lighting the Lamp of Wisdom: A Week Inside a Yoga Ashram
by John Ittner; Foreword by Dr. David Frawley
This insider's guide to Hindu spiritual life takes you into a typical week of retreat inside a yoga ashram to demystify the experience and show you what to expect from your own visit. Includes a discussion of worship services, meditation and yoga classes, chanting and music, work practice, and more.   6 x 9, 192 pp, b/w photographs, Quality PB, ISBN 1-893361-52-7 **$15.95**; HC, ISBN 1-893361-37-3 **$24.95**

Making a Heart for God: A Week Inside a Catholic Monastery
by Dianne Aprile; Foreword by Brother Patrick Hart, ocso
This essential guide to experiencing life in a Catholic monastery takes you to the Abbey of Gethsemani—the Trappist monastery in Kentucky that was home to author Thomas Merton—to explore the details. "More balanced and informative than the popular *The Cloister Walk* by Kathleen Norris." —*Choice: Current Reviews for Academic Libraries*   6 x 9, 224 pp, b/w photographs, Quality PB, ISBN 1-893361-49-7 **$16.95**; HC, ISBN 1-893361-14-4 **$21.95**

Waking Up: A Week Inside a Zen Monastery
by Jack Maguire; Foreword by John Daido Loori, Roshi
An essential guide to what it's like to spend a week inside a Zen Buddhist monastery.
6 x 9, 224 pp, b/w photographs, Quality PB, ISBN 1-893361-55-1 **$16.95**;
HC, ISBN 1-893361-13-6 **$21.95**

Spirituality

Autumn: A Spiritual Biography of the Season
Edited by Gary Schmidt and Susan M. Felch; Illustrations by Mary Azarian
Autumn is a season of fruition and harvest, of thanksgiving and celebration of abundance and goodness of the earth. But it is also a season that starkly and realistically encourages us to see the limitations of our time. Warm and poignant pieces by Wendell Berry, David James Duncan, Robert Frost, A. Bartlett Giamatti, Kimiko Hahn, P. D. James, Julian of Norwich, Garret Keizer, Tracy Kidder, Anne Lamott, May Sarton, and many others rejoice in autumn as a time of preparation and reflection.
6 x 9, 320 pp, 5 b/w illus., Quality PB, ISBN 1-59473-118-7 **$18.99**; HC, ISBN 1-59473-005-9 **$22.99**

Awakening the Spirit, Inspiring the Soul
30 Stories of Interspiritual Discovery in the Community of Faiths
Edited by Brother Wayne Teasdale and Martha Howard, MD; Foreword by Joan Borysenko, PhD
Thirty original spiritual mini-biographies that showcase the varied ways that people come to faith—and what that means—in today's multi-religious world.
6 x 9, 224 pp, HC, ISBN 1-59473-039-3 **$21.99**

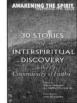

Winter: A Spiritual Biography of the Season
Edited by Gary Schmidt and Susan M. Felch; Illustrations by Barry Moser
Delves into the varied feelings that winter conjures in us, calling up both the barrenness and the beauty of the natural world in wintertime. Includes selections by Will Campbell, Rachel Carson, Annie Dillard, Donald Hall, Ron Hansen, Jane Kenyon, Jamaica Kincaid, Barry Lopez, Kathleen Norris, John Updike, E. B. White, and many others. "This outstanding anthology features top-flight nature and spirituality writers on the fierce, inexorable season of winter.... Remarkably lively and warm, despite the icy subject." —*Publishers Weekly* Starred Review
6 x 9, 288 pp, 6 b/w illus., Deluxe PB w/flaps, ISBN 1-893361-92-6 **$18.95**; HC, ISBN 1-893361-53-5 **$21.95**

The Alphabet of Paradise: An A–Z of Spirituality for Everyday Life
by Howard Cooper 5 x 7¾, 224 pp, Quality PB, ISBN 1-893361-80-2 **$16.95**

Creating a Spiritual Retirement: A Guide to the Unseen Possibilities in Our Lives
by Molly Srode 6 x 9, 208 pp, b/w photos, Quality PB, ISBN 1-59473-050-42 **$14.99**;
HC, ISBN 1-893361-75-6 **$19.95**

The Geography of Faith: Underground Conversations on Religious, Political and Social Change *by Daniel Berrigan and Robert Coles; Updated introduction and afterword by the authors* 6 x 9, 224 pp, Quality PB, ISBN 1-893361-40-3 **$16.95**

God Lives in Glass: Reflections of God for Adults through the Eyes of Children
by Robert J. Landy, PhD; Foreword by Sandy Eisenberg Sasso
7 x 6, 64 pp, HC, Full-color illus., ISBN 1-893361-30-6 **$12.95**

God Within: Our Spiritual Future—As Told by Today's New Adults *Edited by Jon M. Sweeney and the Editors at SkyLight Paths* 6 x 9, 176 pp, Quality PB, ISBN 1-893361-15-2 **$14.95**

Jewish Spirituality: A Brief Introduction for Christians *by Lawrence Kushner*
5½ x 8½, 112 pp, Quality PB, ISBN 1-58023-150-0 **$12.95** *(a Jewish Lights book)*

A Jewish Understanding of the New Testament
by Rabbi Samuel Sandmel; New preface by Rabbi David Sandmel
5½ x 8½, 384 pp, Quality PB, ISBN 1-59473-048-2 **$19.99**

Journeys of Simplicity: Traveling Light with Thomas Merton, Basho, Edward Abbey, Annie Dillard & Others *by Philip Harnden* 5 x 7¼, 128 pp, HC, ISBN 1-893361-76-4 **$16.95**

Keeping Spiritual Balance As We Grow Older: More than 65 Creative Ways to Use Purpose, Prayer, and the Power of Spirit to Build a Meaningful Retirement
by Molly and Bernie Srode 8 x 8, 224 pp, Quality PB, ISBN 1-59473-042-3 **$16.99**

The Monks of Mount Athos: A Western Monk's Extraordinary Spiritual Journey on Eastern Holy Ground *by M. Basil Pennington, ocso; Foreword by Archimandrite Dionysios*
6 x 9, 256 pp, 10+ b/w line drawings, Quality PB, ISBN 1-893361-78-0 **$18.95**

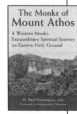

One God Clapping: The Spiritual Path of a Zen Rabbi *by Alan Lew with Sherril Jaffe*
5½ x 8½, 336 pp, Quality PB, ISBN 1-58023-115-2 **$16.95** *(a Jewish Lights book)*

Spiritual Biography—SkyLight Lives

SkyLight Lives reintroduces the lives and works of key spiritual figures of our time—people who by their teaching or example have challenged our assumptions about spirituality and have caused us to look at it in new ways.

  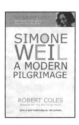 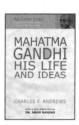

The Life of Evelyn Underhill
An Intimate Portrait of the Groundbreaking Author of *Mysticism*
by Margaret Cropper; Foreword by Dana Greene
Evelyn Underhill was a passionate writer and teacher who wrote elegantly on mysticism, worship, and devotional life. This is the story of how she made her way toward spiritual maturity, from her early days of agnosticism to the years when her influence was felt throughout the world.
6 x 9, 288 pp, 5 b/w photos, Quality PB, ISBN 1-893361-70-5 **$18.95**

Mahatma Gandhi: His Life and Ideas
by Charles F. Andrews; Foreword by Dr. Arun Gandhi
Examines from a contemporary Christian activist's point of view the religious ideas and political dynamics that influenced the birth of the peaceful resistance movement, the primary tool that Gandhi and the people of his homeland would use to gain India its freedom from British rule.
6 x 9, 336 pp, 5 b/w photos, Quality PB, ISBN 1-893361-89-6 **$18.95**

Simone Weil: A Modern Pilgrimage
by Robert Coles
The extraordinary life of the spiritual philosopher who's been called both saint and madwoman. Robert Coles' intriguing study of Weil is an insightful portrait of the beloved and controversial thinker whose life and writings influenced many (from T. S. Eliot to Adrienne Rich to Albert Camus), and continue to inspire seekers everywhere.
6 x 9, 208 pp, Quality PB, ISBN 1-893361-34-9 **$16.95**

Zen Effects: The Life of Alan Watts
by Monica Furlong
Through his widely popular books and lectures, Alan Watts (1915–1973) did more to introduce Eastern philosophy and religion to Western minds than any figure before or since. Here is the first and only full-length biography of one of the most charismatic spiritual leaders of the twentieth century.
6 x 9, 264 pp, Quality PB, ISBN 1-893361-32-2 **$16.95**

More Spiritual Biography

Bede Griffiths: An Introduction to His Interspiritual Thought
by Wayne Teasdale   6 x 9, 288 pp, Quality PB, ISBN 1-893361-77-2 **$18.95**

Inspired Lives: Exploring the Role of Faith and Spirituality in the Lives of Extraordinary People
by Joanna Laufer and Kenneth S. Lewis   6 x 9, 256 pp, Quality PB, ISBN 1-893361-33-0 **$16.95**

Spiritual Innovators: Seventy-Five Extraordinary People Who Changed the World in
the Past Century   *Edited by Ira Rifkin and the Editors at SkyLight Paths; Foreword by Robert Coles*
6 x 9, 304 pp, b/w photographs, Quality PB, ISBN 1-893361-50-0 **$16.95**; HC, ISBN 1-893361-43-8 **$24.95**

White Fire: A Portrait of Women Spiritual Leaders in America
by Rabbi Malka Drucker; Photographs by Gay Block
7 x 10, 320 pp, 30+ b/w photos, HC, ISBN 1-893361-64-0 **$24.95**

Spiritual Poetry—The Mystic Poets

Experience these mystic poets as you never have before. Each beautiful, compact book includes: A brief introduction to the poet's time and place; a summary of the major themes of the poet's mysticism and religious tradition; essential selections from the poet's most important works; and an appreciative preface by a contemporary spiritual writer.

Hafiz: The Mystic Poets
Preface by Ibrahim Gamard
Hafiz is known throughout the world as Persia's greatest poet, with sales of his poems in Iran today only surpassed by those of the Qur'an itself. His probing and joyful verse speaks to people from all backgrounds who long to taste and feel divine love and experience harmony with all living things.
5 x 7¼, 144 pp, HC, ISBN 1-59473-009-1 **$16.99**

Hopkins: The Mystic Poets
Preface by Rev. Thomas Ryan, CSP
Gerard Manley Hopkins, Christian mystical poet, is beloved for his use of fresh language and startling metaphors to describe the world around him. Although his verse is lovely, beneath the surface lies a searching soul, wrestling with and yearning for God.
5 x 7¼, 112 pp, HC, ISBN 1-59473-010-5 **$16.99**

Tagore: The Mystic Poets
Preface by Swami Adiswarananda
Rabindranath Tagore is often considered the "Shakespeare" of modern India. A great mystic, Tagore was the teacher of W. B. Yeats and Robert Frost, the close friend of Albert Einstein and Mahatma Gandhi, and the winner of the Nobel Prize for Literature. This beautiful sampling of Tagore's two most important works, *The Gardener* and *Gitanjali,* offers a glimpse into his spiritual vision that has inspired people around the world.
5 x 7¼, 144 pp, HC, ISBN 1-59473-008-3 **$16.99**

Whitman: The Mystic Poets
Preface by Gary David Comstock
Walt Whitman was the most innovative and influential poet of the nineteenth century. This beautiful sampling of Whitman's most important poetry from *Leaves of Grass,* and selections from his prose writings, offers a glimpse into the spiritual side of his most radical themes—love for country, love for others, and love of Self.
5 x 7¼, 192 pp, HC, ISBN 1-59473-041-5 **$16.99**

Sacred Texts—SkyLight Illuminations Series
Andrew Harvey, series editor

Offers today's spiritual seeker an enjoyable entry into the great classic texts of the world's spiritual traditions. Each classic is presented in an accessible translation, with facing pages of guided commentary from experts, giving you the keys you need to understand the history, context, and meaning of the text. This series enables readers of all backgrounds to experience and understand classic spiritual texts directly, and to make them a part of their lives. Andrew Harvey writes the foreword to each volume, an insightful, personal introduction to each classic.

Bhagavad Gita
Annotated & Explained
Translation by Shri Purohit Swami; Annotation by Kendra Crossen Burroughs
"The very best Gita for first-time readers." —Ken Wilber. Millions of people turn daily to India's most beloved holy book, whose universal appeal has made it popular with non-Hindus and Hindus alike. This edition introduces you to the characters, explains references and philosophical terms, shares the interpretations of famous spiritual leaders and scholars, and more.
5½ x 8½, 192 pp, Quality PB, ISBN 1-893361-28-4 **$16.95**

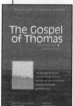

Dhammapada
Annotated & Explained
Translation by Max Müller and revised by Jack Maguire; Annotation by Jack Maguire
The Dhammapada—believed to have been spoken by the Buddha himself over 2,500 years ago—contain most of Buddhism's central teachings. This timeless text concisely and inspirationally portrays the route a person travels as he or she advances toward enlightenment and describes the fundamental role of mental conditioning in making us who we are.
5½ x 8½, 160 pp, b/w photographs, Quality PB, ISBN 1-893361-42-X **$14.95**

The Gospel of Thomas
Annotated & Explained
Translation and annotation by Stevan Davies
Discovered in 1945, this collection of aphoristic sayings sheds new light on the origins of Christianity and the intriguing figure of Jesus, portraying the Kingdom of God as a present fact about the world, rather than a future promise or future threat.
5½ x 8½, 192 pp, Quality PB, ISBN 1-893361-45-4 **$16.95**

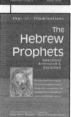

Hasidic Tales
Annotated & Explained
Translation and annotation by Rabbi Rami Shapiro
Introduces the legendary tales of the impassioned Hasidic rabbis, which demonstrate the spiritual power of unabashed joy, offer lessons for leading a holy life, and remind us that the Divine can be found in the everyday.
5½ x 8½, 240 pp, Quality PB, ISBN 1-893361-86-1 **$16.95**

The Hebrew Prophets
Selections Annotated & Explained
Translation and annotation by Rabbi Rami Shapiro
Focuses on the central themes covered by all the Hebrew prophets: moving from ignorance to wisdom, injustice to justice, cruelty to compassion, and despair to joy, and challenges us to engage in justice, kindness, and humility in every aspect of our lives.
5½ x 8½, 224 pp, Quality PB, ISBN 1-59473-037-7 **$16.99**

Sacred Texts—SkyLight Illuminations Series
Andrew Harvey, series editor

The Hidden Gospel of Matthew: Annotated & Explained
Translation and annotation by Ron Miller
Takes you deep into the text cherished around the world to discover the words and events that have the strongest connection to the historical Jesus. Reveals the underlying story of Matthew, a story that transcends the traditional theme of an atoning death and focuses instead on Jesus's radical call for personal transformation and social change.
5½ x 8½, 272 pp, Quality PB, ISBN 1-59473-038-5 **$16.99**

The Secret Book of John
The Gnostic Gospel—Annotated & Explained
Translation and annotation by Stevan Davies
Introduces the most significant and influential text of the ancient Gnostic religion. This central myth of Gnosticism tells the story of how God fell from perfect Oneness to imprisonment in the material world, and how by knowing our divine nature and our divine origins—that we are one with God—we reverse God's descent and find our salvation.
5½ x 8½, 208 pp, Quality PB, ISBN 1-59473-082-2 **$16.99**

Rumi and Islam: Selections from His Stories, Poems, and Discourses—
Annotated & Explained
Translation and annotation by Ibrahim Gamard
Offers a new way of thinking about Rumi's poetry. Focuses on Rumi's place within the Sufi tradition of Islam, providing insight into the mystical side of the religion—one that has love of God at its core and sublime wisdom teachings as its pathways.
5½ x 8½, 240 pp, Quality PB, ISBN 1-59473-002-4 **$15.99**

Selections from the Gospel of Sri Ramakrishna
Annotated & Explained
Translation by Swami Nikhilananda; Annotation by Kendra Crossen Burroughs
The words of India's greatest example of God-consciousness and mystical ecstasy in recent history. Introduces the fascinating world of the Indian mystic and the universal appeal of his message that has inspired millions of devotees for more than a century.
5½ x 8½, 240 pp, b/w photographs, Quality PB, ISBN 1-893361-46-2 **$16.95**

The Way of a Pilgrim: Annotated & Explained
Translation and annotation by Gleb Pokrovsky
This classic of Russian spirituality is the delightful account of one man who sets out to learn the prayer of the heart—also known as the "Jesus prayer"—and how the practice transforms his life.
5½ x 8½, 160 pp, Illus., Quality PB, ISBN 1-893361-31-4 **$14.95**

Zohar: Annotated & Explained
Translation and annotation by Daniel C. Matt
The best-selling author of *The Essential Kabbalah* brings together in one place the most important teachings of the Zohar, the canonical text of Jewish mystical tradition. Guides you step by step through the midrash, mystical fantasy, and Hebrew scripture that make up the Zohar, explaining the inner meanings in facing-page commentary.
5½ x 8½, 176 pp, Quality PB, ISBN 1-893361-51-9 **$15.99**

About SKYLIGHT PATHS Publishing

SkyLight Paths Publishing is creating a place where people of different spiritual traditions come together for challenge and inspiration, a place where we can help each other understand the mystery that lies at the heart of our existence.

Through spirituality, our religious beliefs are increasingly becoming a part of our lives—rather than *apart* from our lives. While many of us may be more interested than ever in spiritual growth, we may be less firmly planted in traditional religion. Yet, we do want to deepen our relationship to the sacred, to learn from our own as well as from other faith traditions, and to practice in new ways.

SkyLight Paths sees both believers and seekers as a community that increasingly transcends traditional boundaries of religion and denomination—people wanting to learn from each other, *walking together, finding the way.*

For your information and convenience, at the back of this book we have provided a list of other SkyLight Paths books you might find interesting and useful. They cover the following subjects:

Buddhism / Zen	Gnosticism	Mysticism
Catholicism	Hinduism /	Poetry
Children's Books	Vedanta	Prayer
Christianity	Inspiration	Religious Etiquette
Comparative	Islam / Sufism	Retirement
Religion	Judaism / Kabbalah /	Spiritual Biography
Current Events	Enneagram	Spiritual Direction
Earth-Based	Meditation	Spirituality
Spirituality	Midrash Fiction	Women's Interest
Global Spiritual	Monasticism	Worship
Perspectives		

Or phone, fax, mail or e-mail to: SKYLIGHT PATHS Publishing
Sunset Farm Offices, Route 4 • P.O. Box 237 • Woodstock, Vermont 05091
Tel: (802) 457-4000 • Fax: (802) 457-4004 • www.skylightpaths.com
Credit card orders: (800) 962-4544 (8:30AM–5:30PM ET Monday–Friday)
Generous discounts on quantity orders. SATISFACTION GUARANTEED. Prices subject to change.